COLLINS GEM

WHALES
& DOLPHINS

Mark Carwardine

D1197772

HarperCollins*Publishers*

HarperCollins Publishers
PO Box, Glasgow G4 0NB

First published 1998
This edition published 1999

Reprint 10 9 8 7 6 5 4 3 2 1 0

ISBN 0 00 472273-6

Printed in Italy by Amadeus S.p.A.

SPECIES DIRECTORY

GREY WHALE

Eschrichtius robustus

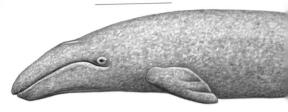

Bᴙ the time the grey whale received official protection, in 1946, it was dangerously close to extinction. After centuries of intensive whaling, the species was already extinct in the North Atlantic

Feeding grey whales, Mexico

and there were probably no more than a few hundred individuals left in the North Pacific. Fortunately, there were enough survivors for the grey whale to make a remarkable comeback – so remarkable, in fact, that its recovery is unmatched by any other species of great whale.

Size: 12–14 m; 15–35 tonnes.
Distribution: Spends winter around Baja California, Mexico, and summer in the Arctic's Bering, Chukchi and western Beaufort seas. Hugging the North American coastline, it migrates between these two seasonal ranges twice every year.
Diet: The bulk of its diet consists of tiny crustaceans, called amphipods, that live in the sediment on the seabed. It occasionally feeds on schooling fish or swarming crustaceans as well.
Status: The current population of 20,000–25,000, in the eastern North Pacific, may even exceed pre-exploitation levels. Recent evidence suggests that there may be a further 200–250 summering in the Sea of Okhotsk.

INCREDIBLE JOURNEYS OF THE GREY WHALE

Grey whales commute up to 10,000 km along the entire length of the North American coastline, and back again, every year. In fact, in a grey whale's lifetime of 40 years or more, it swims the equivalent of a trip to the Moon and back.

Feeding in the Arctic: *April – October*
Grey whales spend every summer in the Bering, Chukchi and western Beaufort seas where, for about five months of the year, they eat as much as they possibly can. They use their mouths like vacuum cleaners and literally suck up sediment from the seabed, sieve this with their baleen plates, and then swallow the tiny crustaceans trapped inside. Each adult grey whale eats nearly 70 tonnes of these little creatures in one summer-long feast. Their aim is to put on enough body weight, in the form of blubber and fat, to survive the rest of the year without food.

Migrating south: *November – February*
Early in October, the whales begin to migrate south. The pregnant females are first to go, followed by non-pregnant females, then mature males, immature females next and, finally, the immature males. They file through Unimak Pass, a narrow gap between islands in the Aleutian chain, and head south. They can cover up to 160 km a day, and the entire journey takes them a couple of months.

Breeding in the sub-tropics: *December – April*
The first to arrive in the breeding lagoons, along the
Pacific coast of Baja California, are the pregnant
females who then give birth to their calves. The
calves drink huge quantities of their mothers' fat-
laden milk and gain weight rapidly. In a race against
time, they have to be fit and ready for their first
journey north within a few months.

Migrating north: *February – June*
The grey whales tend to swim a little slower on
their journey north and the females with calves,
especially, rest for a few hours or even a few days
at a time, until they reach their temporary Arctic
home for another summer.

BOWHEAD WHALE
Balaena mysticetus

THE only large whale to be living exclusively in
the Arctic, the bowhead is well adapted to life
in its freezing home. With a layer of blubber up to
70 cm thick, and an ability to create its own
breathing holes by breaking through the ice, it is
able to live right up to the edge of the Arctic pack
ice. Its head is its most distinctive feature and,
indeed, the enormous bow-shaped skull gives the
bowhead its name. When lying at the surface, in
profile, its triangular head and rounded back make it
resemble the supposed shape of the Loch Ness
Monster.

Size: 14–18 m; 60–100 tonnes.
Distribution: Cold Arctic and sub-Arctic waters,
rarely far from the pack ice. Normally migrates to
the high arctic in summer, but retreats southwards
with the advancing ice edge in winter.
Diet: Krill, copepods and other small- and medium-
sized crustaceans form the bulk of the diet. Recent
evidence suggests that bowheads may also feed
on a variety of other invertebrates on or close to
the seabed.
Status: Heavily hunted by commercial whalers for
several centuries, and still being taken by small-
scale indigenous whalers, the bowhead also
suffers from oil and gas exploration and other
forms of disturbance. The total surviving
population is estimated to be only 6,000–9,000.

NORTHERN AND SOUTHERN RIGHT WHALES

Eubalaena australis (southern); *Eubalaena glacialis* (northern)

W ITH their enormous heads covered in strange, hardened patches of skin, their dark, rounded bodies, and their lack of a dorsal fin, northern and southern right whales look almost identical. But they are believed to be distinct species and, in fact, there are some subtle differences in the structure of their skulls. Right whale calves do not have the strange patches of skin, known as callosities, when they are born; these develop as the animals get older. Scientists take advantage of the callosities to identify individual right whales, because each one has a different arrangement on its head.

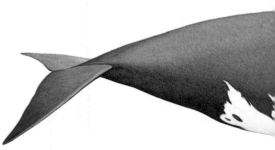

Size: 11–18 m; 30–80 tonnes.

Distribution: The main population of northern right whales is in the western North Atlantic, but there are occasional sightings in the eastern North Atlantic and the eastern North Pacific. The southern right whale breeds in South America, southern Africa and Australasia; its summer feeding grounds are in colder waters towards the Antarctic.

Diet: Copepods are the main food; krill are also sometimes eaten.

Status: The northern right whale is the rarest large whale in the world and is critically endangered; after years of heavy exploitation by whalers it has never recovered. The southern right whale was also heavily depleted, and is still rare, but is showing signs of recovery.

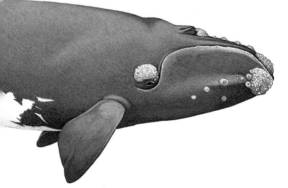

ON THE VERGE OF EXTINCTION

Northern right whales were probably the first whales to be hunted commercially: Basque whalers were killing them in the Bay of Biscay, north of Spain, as early as the 11th century. They continued to be popular targets for commercial whalers for many centuries. Named for being the 'right' whales to catch, they were easy to approach, slow swimmers, lived close to shore, normally floated when dead, and provided large quantities of valuable oil, meat and whalebone. By the early 1900s, both species – northern and southern – were critically close to extinction.

They have been protected since the mid-1930s, but only the southern right whale is showing signs of recovery. The sad fact is that, with just 300-odd survivors, the northern right whale is probably closer to extinction than any other large whale – and may never recover.

Northern right whale, Mexico

PYGMY RIGHT WHALE

Caperea marginata

THE pygmy right whale is the smallest species of baleen whale, and far more streamlined than its closest relatives. It is very poorly known, and rarely seen alive, so most of the information available comes from dead animals caught in fishing nets or washed ashore. Like the other right whales, it has a strongly arched lower jaw – but it differs from them in having a pronounced dorsal fin.

Size: 5.5–6.5 m ; 3–3.5 tonnes.
Distribution: Known from a relatively small number of widely dispersed records across temperate waters of the southern hemisphere. Seems to be most common in New Zealand, southern Australia and South Africa.
Diet: Copepods are believed to be its main food.
Status: The only baleen whale that has not been the target of large-scale commercial whaling, although some animals drown in fishing nets off South Africa. Otherwise, very little is known about its status.

HUMPBACK WHALE

Megaptera novaeangliae

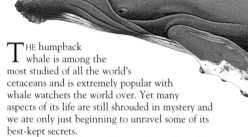

THE humpback whale is among the most studied of all the world's cetaceans and is extremely popular with whale watchers the world over. Yet many aspects of its life are still shrouded in mystery and we are only just beginning to unravel some of its best-kept secrets.

The humpback is well known for its long flippers, which can grow to nearly a third of its length. In fact, the flippers are so outrageously long that they resemble wings and have given the humpback its scientific name, *Megaptera novaeangliae*, which means 'big-winged New Englander' (the first specimen to be formally described, in 1781, came from New England, in the eastern United States).

The humpback's head is also distinctive, with a series of knobs, or tubercles, covering the rostrum and much of the lower jaw; about the size of a golf ball, each knob is a hair follicle with a single, coarse hair growing out of its centre.

Humpbacks are probably the most energetic of all

the large
whales and are
well known for their
spectacular breaching, as
well as lobtailing, flipper-
slapping and spyhopping. Even
when they seem to be resting, they are fun
to watch and may lie on their backs, or sides,
holding their enormous flippers high in the air.
Herman Melville, who mentioned humpbacks
in *Moby Dick*, knew what he was talking about when
he described them as 'the most gamesome and
lighthearted of all the whales, making more gay foam
and whitewater generally than any of them'.

Size: 11.5–15 m; 25–30 tonnes.

Distribution: Widely distributed in all oceans of the world, from the poles to the tropics. Feeds in high latitudes during the spring, summer and early autumn, and migrates to tropical breeding grounds for the winter.

Diet: Schooling fish (including herring, sand lance, capelin, mackerel and salmon) as well as krill and other crustaceans.

Status: Nearly a quarter of a million humpback whales were killed by the whaling industry, wiping out more than 95 per cent of the world population. Fortunately, in recent years, they seem to be making a good recovery in many parts of their range.

Humpback whale lobtailing, Dominican Republic

FISHING WITH NETS OF BUBBLES

Humpback whales have developed an extraordinarily diverse and ingenious range of techniques for catching their food. They lunge through patches of fish or krill with their mouths wide open, literally gulping vast mouthfuls out of the ocean, and even stun their prey with slaps of their flippers or flukes.

But no technique is more impressive than fishing with nets made of bubbles. In the North Atlantic, they tend to use huge, explosive bubble clouds to catch worm-like fish called sand eels, releasing a single blast of bubbles underwater that probably concentrates and disorientates their prey. But to catch herring in the northern North Pacific and Bering Sea they prefer more delicate bubble nets, which strongly resemble man-made seine nets both in design and in the way they are deployed. ▶

Humpback whale lunge-feeding, SE Alaska, USA

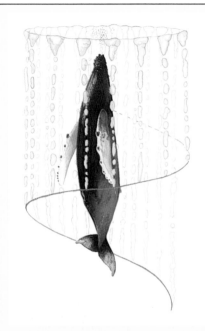

◄ Known simply as 'bubble-clouding', or 'bubble-netting', fishing with bubbles is all the more sensational because the climax of the action takes place in full view above the surface of the water.

When a humpback whale forms a bubble net on its own, it dives beneath a school of fish or krill and starts to release bubbles from its blowholes. Then it swims slowly towards the surface, in a spiral, to form a circular barrier of bubbles around the school. As soon as the 'net' is complete, it swims through the centre with its mouth wide open. The water is flushed out through the baleen plates, as the whale rises above the surface, and the fish or krill trapped inside its mouth are swept up by the tongue and swallowed.

Incredibly, as many as eighteen humpback whales may work together in a more complex form of bubble-net fishing, requiring an almost incomprehensible level of coordination.

It begins with all the members of a fishing group swimming slowly at the surface, spending a few minutes resting and catching their collective breath. Then they all dive and disappear beneath the surface together. No-one knows exactly what happens underwater but, after about five or ten minutes, bubbles begin to break the surface, each one roughly the size of a dinner plate. These form part of a huge circle that can be up to 45 m across. Suddenly, hundreds of tonnes of blubber and gaping mouths erupt from within the circle in one great foaming mass. With water gushing down their distended throat pleats, and fish leaping for their lives, the whales explode to a height of nearly 6 m before sinking back into the depths. It is one of the greatest wildlife spectacles on Earth.

SINGING HUMPBACKS

Drop a hydrophone into the water in an area where
humpback whales are breeding and you may hear a
baffling medley of moans, groans, roars, snores,
squeaks and whistles. These are the unearthly,
hauntingly beautiful sounds made by male
humpback whales, which are famous for singing the
longest and most complex songs in the animal
kingdom.

The singing whales hang almost upside-down in
the water, often fairly close to the surface, with
their eyes closed and their heads pointing towards
the seabed. They sing throughout the day and night
– and may continue for 24 hours or even longer with

hardly a break. Since most of the singing takes place at the breeding grounds, and exclusively by males, it is probably used to woo females and to warn away unwanted competition from rival males. But it is also possible that the songs have more subtle meanings and nuances that we do not yet understand.

A song can last for as long as half an hour and, as soon as the whale has finished, it simply goes back to the beginning and sings the same song all over again. Each song consists of between two and nine main components, which are always sung in the same order but are forever being refined and improved. This means that the song heard one day is quite different to the one being heard several months later. When the whales return to their breeding grounds the following winter, they immediately start singing the version of the song that was in vogue at the end of the previous breeding season.

Even more extraordinary is the fact that all the humpbacks in one area sing broadly the same song, incorporating each other's improvisations as they go along. It is as if they compose and then re-write the 'music' together. In this way, the entire composition changes over a period of about five years.

Meanwhile, humpback whales in other parts of the world sing very different compositions. It is as if the ones living around Hawaii sing in American English, while those living off the coast of Australia, for example, sing in Australian English.

MINKE WHALE

Balaenoptera acutorostrata

THE minke (pronounced mink-ee) is one of the smallest of the baleen whales, and is also the commonest. Named after an 18th century Norwegian whaler, it may have replaced some of its larger and more endangered relatives and, in some areas at least, appears to have increased in number. It is quite

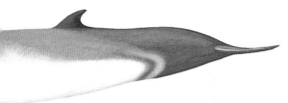

variable in appearance: animals in the northern hemisphere, for example, have a white band on their flippers, but this is absent on many southern hemisphere animals. In some parts of the world, minke whales have learnt to recognise whale-watch boats and often approach to within a metre or so.

Size: 7–10 m; 5–10 tonnes.
Distribution: Virtually worldwide, from the tropics to the edge of the polar ice, although most common in cooler waters. Some are migratory, others appear to be resident. Occurs inshore and, less frequently, offshore.
Diet: Mainly krill and small schooling fish.
Status: The minke whale's small size saved it from commercial whalers until relatively recently. However, now that most of its larger relatives are endangered and officially protected, it is the only baleen whale being hunted commercially under the auspices of the IWC. Nevertheless, it is still the most abundant of all baleen whales.

BRYDE'S WHALE

Balaenoptera edeni

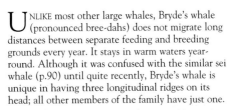

UNLIKE most other large whales, Bryde's whale (pronounced bree-dahs) does not migrate long distances between separate feeding and breeding grounds every year. It stays in warm waters year-round. Although it was confused with the similar sei whale (p.90) until quite recently, Bryde's whale is unique in having three longitudinal ridges on its head; all other members of the family have just one.

Size: 11.5–14.5 m; 12–20 tonnes.

Distribution: Warm waters worldwide. Rarely moving further north or south than 40°, it occurs both offshore and near the coast. There seem to be specific pockets of abundance, such as off South Africa, Sri Lanka, Japan, Fiji and western Australia, although this may reflect research effort as much as distribution.

Diet: Mainly schooling fish, but also squid and crustaceans.

Status: The history of whaling for Bryde's whale is largely unknown, because it was not consistently distinguished from the similar sei whale until quite recently. However, it is likely that some populations have been depleted by whaling.

SEI WHALE
Balaenoptera borealis

THE sei whale (pronounced say) is poorly known compared with most other baleen whales. It lives far from shore, tends to be elusive, and does not seem to gather in the same specific areas year after year. No commercial whale-watch operation relies on this species, for example, although it is sometimes encountered during tours specialising in humpbacks, minkes and other large whales. Named after a Norwegian word for the fish we call pollack, for many years it was confused with Bryde's whale (p.88), which is quite similar. As with all six members of the sei whale's family, females are slightly larger than males and animals in the southern hemisphere tend to be larger than those in the northern hemisphere.

Size: 12–16 m; 20–30 tonnes.
Distribution: Mainly in deep, temperate waters
worldwide, but also found in the sub-tropics and
tropics. Rarely seen close to shore, except in deep
water around islands, and most common in the
southern hemisphere.
Diet: Small crustaceans, such as krill and copepods,
and schooling fish.
Status: Heavily depleted by commercial whaling in
some areas and, as a result, the world population
has dropped from an estimated quarter of a million
to fewer than 60,000.

FIN WHALE

Balaenoptera physalus

FIN whales are unusual in having asymmetrical pigmentation on their heads. The lower 'lip', mouth cavity and some of the baleen plates are white on the right side, but they are uniformly grey or black on the left side. No-one knows the reason for such intriguing coloration, but it is likely to be an adaptation for

feeding, perhaps to confuse the whale's small prey. The second largest animal on earth, the fin whale is a sleek and fast swimmer, capable of reaching speeds of over 30 km/h. It tends to be more social than some other members of the family, and often gathers in small groups.

Size: 18–22 m; 30–80 tonnes.
Distribution: Deep water in tropical, temperate and polar regions worldwide, but most common in cooler waters and in the southern hemisphere. Some populations seem to be resident year-round, but others may migrate between warm waters in winter and cooler waters in summer. Normally encountered offshore, but will approach the coast in deep water.
Diet: A variety of schooling fish, krill and other crustaceans and, to a lesser extent, squid.
Status: The world population was substantially reduced by commercial whalers and, although it is not believed to be in immediate danger, the population has dropped to an estimated 120,000 animals.

BLUE WHALE
Balaenoptera musculus

ONE of the largest animals
ever to have lived on Earth, the blue
is almost as long as a Boeing 737 and weighs
nearly as much as 2,000 people. Its tail flukes alone
are roughly as wide as a soccer goal and its blow is
no less than three storeys high. It needs so much
food that, in terms of weight, it could eat a fully-
grown African elephant every day. Sadly, the sheer
size of the blue whale made it one of the most

sought after species during the heyday of whaling and, in total, it is estimated that more than 350,000 were killed worldwide. There are believed to be three different sub-species: the largest lives in the Antarctic; a slightly smaller one lives in the northern hemisphere; and an even smaller one, known as the pygmy blue whale, lives mainly in tropical waters of the southern hemisphere.

Size: 21–27 m; 100–120 tonnes.
Distribution: Worldwide, from the tropics to the poles, although its distribution is very patchy. Some populations migrate long distances between low-latitude winter breeding grounds and high-latitude summer feeding grounds, but others appear to be resident.
Diet: Various species of krill.
Status: The blue whale was hunted relentlessly from the late nineteenth century until beyond the middle of the twentieth century. So many were killed that some stocks may never recover. Others, such as those off California and Mexico, have begun to show encouraging signs of recovery.

SPERM WHALE
Physeter macrocephalus

THE sperm whale is easily recognised by its huge, squarish head, its wrinkly, prune-like skin, and its uniquely angled, bushy blow. Males are considerably larger than females and the two sexes normally live together only during the breeding season. At other times, there are two main groupings: 'bachelor schools', containing non-breeding males, and 'nursery schools', containing females with calves of

both sexes. When a mother is hungry and needs to dive to the ocean depths for food, she leaves her calf at the surface, where it is looked after by another female. Older males sometimes live alone.

Size: 11–18 m; 20–50 tonnes.
Distribution: Patchy distribution worldwide, from the tropics to high latitudes near the edge of the pack ice. Normally, only large males venture to the extreme north and south of the range. Prefers deep water and usually found offshore, but also occurs over submarine canyons near the coast.
Diet: Squid are the main prey, although octopuses and a wide variety of large fish are also taken.
Status: The sperm whale was the mainstay of the whaling industry, and huge numbers were killed over several centuries. But, against all the odds, it is still fairly numerous and is probably the most abundant of all the great whales.

THE WHALE THAT THINKS IT IS A SUBMARINE

Sperm whales behave more like submarines than air-breathing mammals. They can dive deeper, and for longer, than any other mammal.

They eat as much as a tonne of food every day, each prey animal ranging in size from a few centimetres to almost the length of the whales themselves. One individual was observed tackling a giant squid some 14.5 m long, including its tentacles, while no fewer than 28,000 smaller squid were found in the stomach of another.

In 1991, near the island of Dominica, in the Caribbean, a male sperm whale was recorded making a record-breaking dive to a depth of 2,000 m, and there is circumstantial evidence to suggest they may be able to dive to depths of at least 3,000 m. The longest dive was also recorded in the

Caribbean, in 1983, when five sperm whales surfaced after at least 2 hours 18 minutes underwater.

One explanation for such astonishing diving capabilities may lie in the sperm whale's enormous, barrel-shaped head. Much of the bulk of the head consists of a strange spongy tissue, known as the spermaceti organ, which is filled with a yellowy wax. According to one theory, this could be used to control the whale's buoyancy in the water. In a complicated system involving swapping around cold seawater and warm blood, the whale may be able to alter the temperature – and thus the density – of the wax. If the theory is correct, this could help the whale to sink or float with the minimum of effort.

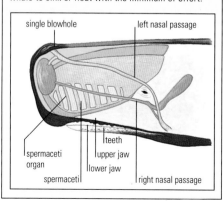

single blowhole

left nasal passage

teeth

upper jaw

lower jaw

spermaceti organ

spermaceti

right nasal passage

DWARF AND PYGMY SPERM WHALES

Kogia simus (dwarf); *Kogia breviceps* (pygmy)

DWARF and pygmy sperm whales are both deep divers, like their much larger and better-known relative, the sperm whale (p.96). They are difficult to tell apart at sea, except at very close range, and have even been mistaken for sharks because of their underslung lower jaws and unusual white markings on either side of the head that resemble gill-slits. The dwarf sperm whale was not recognised as a separate species until 1966.

Dwarf sperm whale

Size: 2.1–2.7 m, 135–275 kg (dwarf); 2.7–3.4 m, 315–400 kg (pygmy).

Distribution: Both species appear to occur worldwide in tropical, sub-tropical and warm temperate waters, although they have never been officially recorded across vast areas within this assumed range. They prefer deep water.

Diet: Both species feed primarily on deep water squid, but will also take a variety of fish, cuttlefish and crustaceans.

Status: Sometimes killed in Japan and other parts of Asia, and unknown numbers are drowned in fishing nets. Neither species appears to be particularly numerous although the pygmy sperm whale, in particular, may be more common than the lack of evidence currently suggests.

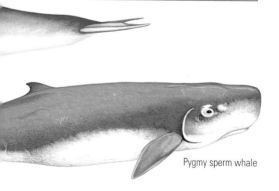

Pygmy sperm whale

NARWHAL

Monodon monoceros

CENTURIES ago, the male narwhal's long, spiralling tusk was believed to be the horn of the legendary unicorn. It is actually a modified tooth, which appears to be used in fights over females and as a visual display of strength. A small number of males have two tusks and, rarely, females grow them as well.

Size: 3.8–5 m; 0.8–1.6 tonnes.

Distribution: Living mostly above the Arctic Circle, and right to the edge of the ice-cap, it spends much of its life navigating through pack ice. Rarely observed in Alaska, the eastern Russian Arctic or the western Canadian Arctic.

Diet: A variety of fish, squid and crustaceans.

Status: Narwhals have been hunted for centuries by indigenous peoples and, until recently, were hunted commercially by several different countries. Oil and gas exploration and pollution are threats in some areas. The total population is believed to be 25,000–45,000.

BELUGA

Delphinapterus leucas

ANCIENT mariners used to call the beluga the 'sea canary' because of its great repertoire of trills, moos, clicks, squeaks and twitters. It can even be heard from above the surface. Not all belugas are white: the body colour changes with age, from dark slate-grey at birth to pure white when the animal is sexually mature at five or ten years old.

Size: *c.*3–5 m; 0.4–1.5 tonnes.

Distribution: Found only in seasonally ice-covered waters of the sub-Arctic and Arctic. Mostly in shallow coastal waters, but will enter estuaries and even rivers.

Diet: A wide variety of fish, as well as crustaceans, squid, octopus and molluscs. Believed to feed mostly on or near the bottom.

Status: Belugas have been hunted for centuries. Pollution is a serious threat in some regions. Appears to be locally common with a total population of around 50,000–70,000.

BEAKED WHALES

THE beaked whales are the strangest and least known of all the cetaceans. Most of the information we have about them has been gleaned from dead animals washed ashore or, in some cases, from a few brief encounters at sea – and several species have never even been seen alive.

There are 21 known species, all belonging to the family Ziphiidae. This includes a new beaked whale from Chile, which was formally identified and named as recently as 1996 (p.118). It is likely that others have yet to be discovered. They are small to medium-sized whales, ranging in length from just under 4 m to nearly 13 m.

Their most remarkable feature is their teeth. In most of the males, there are only two or four teeth in the lower jaw, and none in the upper jaw, while the majority of females have no visible teeth or none at all. Gray's and Shepherd's beaked whales are the main exceptions: they have extra rows of tiny teeth erupting in both sexes. This extraordinary lack of dentition may be an adaptation for feeding on squid, which is their favourite prey, although some members of the family also eat deep-sea fish.

Arnoux's beaked whale

Arnoux's Beaked Whale
Berardius arnuxii

A very poorly known whale, resembling Baird's beaked whale so closely it has been suggested that the two belong to the same species.

Size: 7.8–9.7 m; 7–10 tonnes.
Distribution: Deep offshore waters in the Tasman Sea and elsewhere in the southern hemisphere south of 34°S.

Baird's Beaked Whale
Berardius bairdii

THE largest member of the family and better known than its almost identical relative, Arnoux's beaked whale.

Size: 10.7–12.8 m; c.11–15 tonnes.
Distribution: Deep temperate and sub-arctic waters in the North Pacific.

Baird's beaked whale

NORTHERN BOTTLENOSE WHALE

Hyperoodon ampullatus

ONE of the better known beaked whales, the northern bottlenose is a curious animal and frequently approaches stationary boats for a closer look. Its most distinctive feature is its bulbous forehead.

> **Size:** 7–9 m; 5.8–7.5 tonnes.
> **Distribution:** Deep waters in the northern North Atlantic.

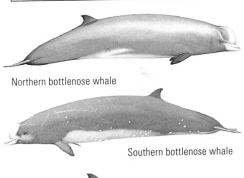

Northern bottlenose whale

Southern bottlenose whale

Sowerby's beaked whale

SOUTHERN BOTTLENOSE WHALE

Hyperoodon planifrons

COMPARED with its northern counterpart, the southern bottlenose is rarely encountered at sea and is relatively poorly known.

Size: 6–7.5 m; *c.*6–8 tonnes.
Distribution: Cold, deep waters of the southern hemisphere, mainly south of 30°S.

SOWERBY'S BEAKED WHALE

Mesoplodon bidens

THE first of the beaked whales to be discovered (in the Moray Firth, Scotland, in 1800), this whale is rarely encountered at sea and is still poorly known.

Size: 4–5 m; 1–1.3 tonnes.
Distribution: Mainly temperate and sub-arctic waters of the northern North Atlantic, especially in the east.

Andrew's Beaked Whale

Mesoplodon bowdoini

A rather distinctive looking whale: the male has a large tooth perched on the top of each side of its highly arched mouthline.

Size: *c.*4–4.7 m; 1–1.5 tonnes.
Distribution: Known only from strandings along the southern coast of Australia (including Tasmania) and New Zealand.

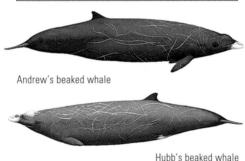

Andrew's beaked whale

Hubb's beaked whale

Blainville's beaked whale

HUBB'S BEAKED WHALE
Mesoplodon carlhubbsi

RECOGNISABLE by its raised white 'cap', strongly arched mouthline, and long, stocky beak, this is one of the few members of the family that may be positively identified at sea.

> **Size:** 5–5.3 m; 1–1.5 tonnes.
> **Distribution:** Most records from California, but also known from Japan and may range right across the North Pacific.

BLAINVILLE'S BEAKED WHALE
Mesoplodon densirostris

RECORDED in all the world's oceans, this whale has a wider distribution than almost any other beaked whale, but sightings are still relatively rare.

> **Size:** 4.5–6 m; *c.*1 tonne.
> **Distribution:** Mainly around the Atlantic coast of the USA, but patchy records from all over the world.

GERVAIS' BEAKED WHALE
Mesoplodon europaeus

LIKE many other members of the family, male
Gervais' beaked whales are covered in scratches
and scars, probably caused by the teeth of other
males during fights.

Size: 4.5–5.2 m; *c.*1–2 tonnes.
Distribution: Deep sub-tropical and warm
    temperate waters in the western North Atlantic,
    with scattered records elsewhere in both the
    North and South Atlantic.

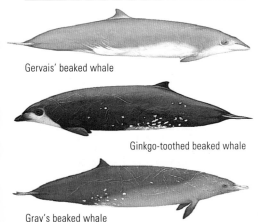

Gervais' beaked whale

Ginkgo-toothed beaked whale

Gray's beaked whale

GINKGO-TOOTHED BEAKED WHALE
Mesoplodon ginkgodens

S O-NAMED because the male's strangely flattened teeth are shaped like the leaves of a ginkgo tree. This whale is less heavily scarred than most other members of the family.

Size: 4.7–5.2 m; *c.*1.5–2 tonnes.
Distribution: Known only from a small number of widely scattered records in the warm waters of the Pacific and Indian Oceans.

GRAY'S BEAKED WHALE
Mesoplodon grayi

T HIS whale seems to be more active at the surface than other beaked whales, and may live in larger groups: in 1874, 28 animals stranded together in the Chatham Islands, east of New Zealand.

Size: 4.5–5.6 m; 1–1.5 tonnes.
Distribution: Cool, temperate waters of the southern hemisphere, mainly south of 30°S.

HECTOR'S BEAKED WHALE

Mesoplodon hectori

THIS whale is known mostly from skeletons and skulls: few have been examined in the flesh and even fewer have been seen alive.

Size: 4–4.5 m; *c.*1–2 tonnes.
Distribution: Cool, temperate waters around New Zealand and elsewhere in the southern hemisphere; possibly also in the North Pacific.

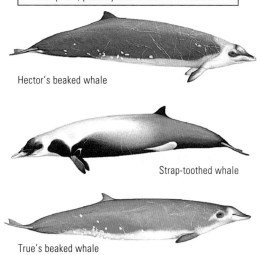

Hector's beaked whale

Strap-toothed whale

True's beaked whale

STRAP-TOOTHED WHALE
Mesoplodon layardii

THE male has two extraordinary teeth which grow from its lower jaw, curl upwards and backwards and then extend over the top of its upper jaw. In older animals, they sometimes meet in the middle, forming a muzzle and preventing the whale from opening its jaws properly. It probably uses its mouth like a vacuum cleaner to suck the prey inside.

Size: 5–6.2 m; *c.*1–3 tonnes.
Distribution: Cool, temperate waters of the southern hemisphere, roughly between 30°S and the Antarctic Convergence.

TRUE'S BEAKED WHALE
Mesoplodon mirus

LIKE other beaked whales in the genus *Mesoplodon*, this whale has a 'flipper pocket' on either side of its body. When swimming, it is believed to tuck its flippers away in these small depressions in the body wall.

Size: 4.9–5.3 m; *c.*1–1.5 tonnes.
Distribution: Mostly known from the western North Atlantic, but also recorded in the eastern North Atlantic, South Africa and Australasia.

STEJNEGER'S BEAKED WHALE
Mesoplodon stejnegeri

DESPITE its alternative name, the Bering Sea beaked whale, this whale prefers deep water and probably avoids much of the relatively shallow Bering Sea.

Size: 5–5.3 m; 1–1.5 tonnes.
Distribution: Cold temperate and sub-arctic waters of the North Pacific (especially around the Aleutian Islands) and in the Sea of Japan.

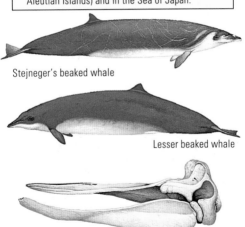

Stejneger's beaked whale

Lesser beaked whale

Longman's beaked whale

LESSER BEAKED WHALE

Mesoplodon peruvianus

THE smallest member of the family and one of the most recent cetacean species to be named. The first complete specimen was found in 1985, at a fish market just south of Lima, in Peru; and the new species was officially named in 1991.

Size: *c.*3.4–3.7 m; weight unknown.
Distribution: Limited records suggest mid- to deep waters in the Eastern Tropical Pacific, mainly off the coast of Peru.

LONGMAN'S BEAKED WHALE

Mesoplodon (Indopacetus) pacificus

ONE of the least known of all the world's cetaceans. The only firm evidence for its existence comes from two weathered skulls: one discovered in 1882 in Queensland, Australia, and the second in 1955 in Somalia. Recently, more than 40 sightings of a new 'beaked' whale species in the western Indian and Pacific oceans have been attributed to this species.

Size: *c.*7–9 m; weight unknown.
Distribution: Uncertain; possibly deep tropical waters of the western Indian and Pacific Oceans.

BAHAMONDE'S BEAKED WHALE

Mesoplodon bahamondi Not Illustrated

A strange skull, belonging to an immature beaked whale, was found on Robinson Crusoe Island, in the Juan Fernández islands off Chile, in June 1986. After nearly a decade of painstaking examination by a group of the world's leading beaked whale experts, Bahamonde's beaked whale was officially named in 1996 – making it the most recent cetacean to be formally recognised as a new species. It is possible that Bahamonde's beaked whale and the unidentified beaked whale (p.117) belong to the same species. But until dead specimens of the unidentified beaked whale are found, there is no way of knowing for sure.

Size: It is estimated that the only skull belonged to an animal some 5.0–5.5 m in length. Weight unknown.

Distribution: Currently known only from the Juan Fernández Archipelago, situated some 590 km to the west of mainland Chile.

UNIDENTIFIED BEAKED WHALE

Mesoplodon sp. 'A'

THIS whale is known only from about 30 positive sightings in the Eastern Tropical Pacific. But no stranded or dead specimens have been available for close examination so it has yet to be properly named.

> **Size:** *c*.5–5.5 m; weight unknown.
> **Distribution:** Mainly known from deep, offshore regions of the Eastern Tropical Pacific, especially in very warm water.

Unidentified beaked whale

Shepherd's beaked whale (see p.118)

Cuvier's beaked whale (see p.118)

SHEPHERD'S BEAKED WHALE
Tasmacetus shepherdi

T HE only beaked whale with a full set of functional teeth (Gray's beaked whale (p.111) has tiny, vestigial teeth in the upper jaw). These occur in both jaws of both sexes, although only the male has a pair of larger teeth at the tip of the lower jaw. *Illustrated on p.117.*

> **Size:** 6–7 m; c.2–3 tonnes.
> **Distribution:** Most records from New Zealand, but also known from elsewhere in the southern hemisphere.

CUVIER'S BEAKED WHALE
Ziphius cavirostris

A LTHOUGH it is probably one of the most abundant and widespread of the beaked whales, Cuvier's beaked whale is surprisingly rarely observed at sea. *Illustrated on p.117.*

> **Size:** 5.5–7 m; 2–3 tonnes.
> **Distribution:** Widely distributed in deep tropical, sub-tropical and temperate waters around the world, especially around oceanic islands and in enclosed seas.

PYGMY KILLER WHALE

Feresa attenuata

THIS whale is believed to prey on other small cetaceans in the wild and has been quite aggressive towards people in captivity. Some individuals have a distinctive white 'chin', but others merely have white 'lips'. Very little is known about this species and, since it tends to avoid boats, it is rarely encountered at sea.

Size: 2.1–2.6 m; *c.*110–170 kg.

Distribution: Deep, offshore waters in the sub-tropics and tropics. Rarely close to shore, except around oceanic islands.

Diet: Mostly fish and squid, although known to attack other dolphins.

Status: Small numbers drowned in fishing nets and caught up in drive fisheries in Japan, Sri Lanka and elsewhere. Its status is unknown, but it does not appear to be common.

MELON-HEADED WHALE

Peponocephala electra

DESPITE its wide distribution, this whale is rarely encountered at sea and is poorly known. Named for its pointed, melon-shaped head, it is a highly social animal and tends to live in large herds. It often creates a lot of spray as it surfaces, and frequently changes direction underwater, making it difficult to see any detail.

Size: 2.1–2.7 m; *c.*160 kg.
Distribution: Sub-tropical and tropical waters worldwide. Usually encountered offshore, and around oceanic islands, and seldom ventures close to land.
Diet: Squid and various small fish.
Status: Some drown in fishing nets, and unknown numbers are hunted in Japan and elsewhere. Its status is unknown, but it does not appear to be particularly common.

FALSE KILLER WHALE

Pseudorca crassidens

THIS whale can look rather menacing, with its black, torpedo-shaped body, and it is known to attack groups of small cetaceans. Yet, in many ways, it behaves more like a dolphin. It leaps high into the air, makes rapid turns underwater, and even rides the bow waves of passing ships.

Size: 4.3–6 m; 1.1–2.2 tonnes.

Distribution: Widely distributed in tropical, sub-tropical and warm temperate waters worldwide. Prefers deep water and normally encountered offshore.

Diet: Mainly fish and squid; also known to attack dolphins.

Status: Small numbers drown in fishing nets, or are hunted for food. Others are shot or driven ashore by fishermen, especially in Japan, who regard them as competitors. A few are also captured for marine parks. Total numbers are unknown, although it does not appear to be particularly common.

LONG-FINNED AND SHORT-FINNED PILOT WHALES

Globicephala melas (long-finned)
Globicephala macrorhynchus (short-finned)

LONG-FINNED and short-finned pilot whales are almost impossible to tell apart at sea, but there is relatively little overlap in their range. The main differences are in the length of the flippers, the shape of the skull and the number of teeth. They are social animals, living in family pods, and are often found in the company of other whales and dolphins. The long-finned pilot whale is one of the species most often involved in mass strandings.

Short-finned pilot whale

Long-finned pilot whale

Size: 3.8–6 m, 1.8–3.5 tonnes (long-finned); 3.6–6.5 m, 1–4 tonnes (short-finned).

Distribution: The long-finned pilot whale has two distinct populations: cool waters of the southern hemisphere and cool waters of the North Atlantic. The short-finned pilot whale prefers warmer waters and is found worldwide. Both species prefer deep water.

Diet: Both species feed mainly on squid.

Status: Large numbers of long-finned pilot whales are killed every year in the Faroe Islands (see p.57–8) and smaller numbers in other parts of the world. Smaller numbers of short-finned pilot whales are killed in Japan, the Caribbean and elsewhere. Both species are still fairly common in many parts of their range.

KILLER WHALE OR ORCA

Orcinus orca

THE killer whale's name is rather confusing. It is not a whale, as such, but the largest member of the dolphin family; and it certainly does not deserve its killer reputation. It is no different from other top predators, such as lions, tigers and polar bears, except that it never hunts people. No-one knows why it should make an exception. Yet there has only ever been one verified 'attack' in the wild – and that was on a surfer, who survived after the whale realised its mistake and spat him out. In fact, many people have swum and kayaked with wild killer whales, with no hint of aggression.

Killer whale playing
'cat-and-mouse' with
sea lion pup, Argentina

Size: 5.5–9.8 m; 2.6–9 tonnes.
Distribution: Despite its rather patchy distribution,
    the killer whale is one of the most wide-ranging
    mammals on earth. It occurs in all seas and
    oceans, from the equator to the poles and from
    near the coast to far offshore (although it prefers
    cooler inshore waters).
Diet: Squid, fish, sea turtles, birds and marine
    mammals. No animal is too large – even adult
    blue whales are hunted on occasion. Pods tend to
    specialise.
Status: Shot by fishermen in some parts of the
    world. Live captures for oceanaria have occurred
    in several countries, most recently Japan and
    Russia. Seems to be fairly common in some parts
    of its range.

TUCUXI
Sotalia fluviatilis

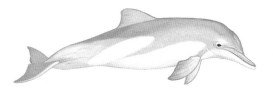

THERE are two main forms of tucuxi (pronounced too-koosh-ee): one found in lakes and rivers, and the other in the sea. Usually known by the first part of its scientific name – 'Sotalia' – it is often seen in the company of Amazon river dolphins (p.159).

Size: 1.3–1.8 m; 35–45 kg.

Distribution: Shallow coastal waters, rivers and lakes of north-eastern South America and eastern Central America. Riverine populations are found as far as 2,500 km up the Amazon.

Diet: A variety of fish and crustaceans (marine and riverine populations have different diets).

Status: As well as hunting and conflicts with fisheries, the damming of the Amazon, mangrove degradation and coastal pollution are all threats to the tucuxi. Still fairly common in some areas.

LONG-SNOUTED SPINNER DOLPHIN

Stenella longirostris

ONE of the most acrobatic of all dolphins, and
named for its incredibly high spinning leaps. It
can spin round on its longitudinal axis as many as
seven times before splashing back into the water.
There are many different varieties of long-snouted
spinner, which vary greatly in body shape, size and
colour depending on where they live.

Size: 1.3–2.1 m; 50–90 kg.
Distribution: Mainly tropical and sub-tropical
waters worldwide, although sometimes occurs in
warm temperate waters as well.
Diet: A variety of mid-water fish and squid.
Status: Numbers reduced significantly by tuna
fishing in the Eastern Tropical Pacific. Many
hunted or drowned in gill nets every year in the
Caribbean, Australia, Japan, the Philippines, Sri
Lanka and Thailand. Still fairly common in some
areas.

SHORT-SNOUTED SPINNER DOLPHIN

Stenella clymene

Not officially classified as a separate species until 1981; until then, it was considered to be one of the many variations of the long-snouted spinner dolphin (p.127).

Size: 1.7–2 m; 50–90 kg.

Distribution: Found in warm temperate, sub-tropical and tropical waters of the Atlantic Ocean, although its precise distribution is poorly known. Mainly occurs in deep water offshore.

Diet: Small fish and squid.

Status: Little known about its status, although it is likely that some hunting takes place in the Caribbean, and unknown numbers are drowned in a variety of fishing nets.

Striped Dolphin

Stenella coeruleoalba

A highly conspicuous animal, which seems to spend an inordinate amount of its time in the air. Its acrobatic repertoire includes high breaches, belly-flops, back somersaults, tail spins, and upside-down porpoising. Its distinctive stripes, and the speed at which it swims, prompted fishermen to call it the 'streaker'.

Size: 1.8–2.5 m; 90–150 kg.
Distribution: Worldwide, mainly in tropical, sub-tropical and warm temperate waters. Usually encountered in deep water.
Diet: Small squid, fish and crustaceans.
Status: Hunted in some regions of the world, especially in a large Japanese drive fishery, and considerable numbers were taken in the Eastern Tropical Pacific tuna-fishing industry until quite recently. Still believed to be fairly common.

PANTROPICAL SPOTTED DOLPHIN

Stenella attenuata

TUNA-FISHING operations in the Eastern Tropical Pacific killed millions of pantropical spotted dolphins in the 1960s, 1970s and 1980s, reducing the regional population by as much as 75 per cent. New laws and release techniques have reduced the level of the slaughter dramatically.

Size: 1.7–2.4 m; 90–115 kg.
Distribution: Widely distributed in warm waters of the Atlantic, Pacific and Indian Oceans, both inshore and offshore. Most abundant nearer the equator, but occurs as far north as 40°N and as far south as 40°S.
Diet: Squid and fish, possibly some crustaceans.
Status: Huge numbers killed by the tuna industry, and smaller numbers in a variety of fisheries in other parts of the world. Still appears to be common in other parts of its range.

ATLANTIC SPOTTED DOLPHIN
Stenella frontalis

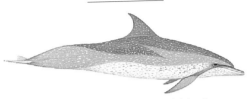

ONE particular population of this dolphin has
been studied in great detail – on Little Bahama
Bank, north of the Bahamas – but the species is
poorly known elsewhere. Young animals have no
spots but these begin to appear as they grow older;
some elderly animals have so many large spots that
the normal background colour of their bodies is
barely visible.

Size: 1.7–2.3 m; 100–140 kg.
Distribution: North and South Atlantic, in warm
  temperate, sub-tropical and tropical waters. Deep,
  offshore animals tend to be smaller and less
  spotted than those living over the continental
  shelf.
Diet: Fish and squid.
Status: Hunted in some areas, and unknown
  numbers are drowned in fishing nets, but still
  appears to be fairly common over much of its
  range.

ATLANTIC HUMP-BACKED DOLPHIN

Sousa teuszii

Astrange-looking animal with a conspicuous, elongated hump on its back. The dorsal fin sits on top of the hump, giving it a rather top-heavy appearance.

Size: 2–2.5 m; 100–150 kg.

Distribution: Found only in the coastal waters of tropical and sub-tropical West Africa. It seems to prefer shallow water, especially around estuaries and mangrove swamps. Known to enter the Niger and some other rivers.

Diet: Mullet and a variety of other fish. Sometimes joins bottlenose dolphins and fishermen in Mauritania, in a joint effort to herd and catch fish.

Status: Some hunting and incidental capture in fishing nets, and mangrove destruction is also a threat. Still appears to be locally common, although its numbers are poorly known.

INDO-PACIFIC HUMP-BACKED DOLPHIN

Sousa chinensis

THIS dolphin varies greatly in appearance, depending on where it lives. The animals west of Sumatra, in Indonesia, have a fatty hump on their backs and a relatively small dorsal fin, whereas those living east and south of Sumatra have no hump but a more prominent dorsal fin. There are also several distinct colour variations.

Size: 2–2.8 m; 150–200 kg.

Distribution: Shallow, coastal waters from northern Australia and southern China in the east, around the entire Indian Ocean, to southern Africa in the west. Mainly in tropical and sub-tropical waters and close to shore.

Diet: Coastal, estuarine and reef fish.

Status: Some hunting and incidental capture in fishing nets may threaten certain local populations, but still appears to be fairly common in parts of its range.

NORTHERN RIGHTWHALE DOLPHIN

Lissodelphis borealis

THE only dolphin in the North Pacific without a dorsal fin. It is a fast swimmer, making low-angled leaps and belly flops and leaving the overall impression of a bouncing motion. Each leap can be an incredible 7 m long.

Size: 2–3 m; *c.*60–100 kg.

Distribution: Cool and warm temperate regions of the northern North Pacific, mainly in deep, offshore waters between 30°N and 50°N. May venture further south if water temperatures are unusually low.

Diet: Mainly squid and lanternfish.

Status: Large numbers drowned in Japanese, Taiwanese and Korean squid driftnet fisheries, and smaller numbers in fishing operations elsewhere. Still appears to be fairly common over much of its range.

SOUTHERN RIGHTWHALE DOLPHIN

Lissodelphis peronii

THE only dolphin in the southern hemisphere without a dorsal fin, this species is very distinctive with its striking black and white body pattern. Despite its remote, offshore distribution, it is fairly easy to see in the right areas and will sometimes even bow-ride.

> **Size:** 1.8–2.9 m; *c.*60–100 kg.
> **Distribution:** Deep, cold temperate to sub-Antarctic waters of the southern hemisphere. The southern limit appears to be the Antarctic Convergence. Rarely seen near land, except in sufficiently deep water.
> **Diet:** Fish (lanternfish seem to be a particular favourite) and squid.
> **Status:** Seems to be fairly common throughout its range and, although small numbers may be killed in South America and some drown in fishing nets, probably not under immediate threat.

SHORT-BEAKED AND LONG-BEAKED COMMON DOLPHINS

Delphinus delphis (short-beaked);
Delphinus capensis (long-beaked)

THERE are many different variations of common dolphin and as many as twenty different species have been proposed over the years. They all have the distinctive hourglass pattern of white, grey, yellow and black on their sides, but they show many differences within this basic framework. In 1995, though, the common dolphin was officially separated into two distinct species, now known as the short-beaked common dolphin and the long-beaked common dolphin. These show many subtle genetic, physical and behavioural differences although they can still be very difficult to tell apart at sea.

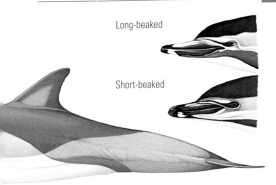

Long-beaked

Short-beaked

Size: 1.7–2.4 m; 70–110 kg.

Distribution: Worldwide in warm temperate, sub-tropical and tropical waters, mainly offshore but also close to the coast. Found in the Red Sea, the Mediterranean and other enclosed seas. Rarely above 60°N in the North Atlantic, 50°N in the North Pacific, and 50°S in the southern hemisphere.

Diet: Small schooling fish and squid.

Status: Huge numbers were killed by Turkish and Russian fishermen in the Black Sea, severely depleting the population. Unknown numbers are drowned in fishing nets worldwide, and local populations seem to be declining in some areas. Otherwise, still fairly common over much of its range.

ROUGH-TOOTHED DOLPHIN

Steno bredanensis

A strange-looking dolphin, with a slightly reptilian appearance to its head, this species is named for a series of fine, vertical wrinkles on the enamel cap of each tooth. The light-coloured blotches on its body may be caused by the bites of cookie-cutter sharks.

Size: 2.1–2.6 m; 100–150 kg.
Distribution: Deep oceanic waters in the tropics, sub-tropics and warm temperate regions of the world. Rarely ranges north of 40°N or south of 35°S.
Diet: Fish, squid and octopus, and possibly molluscs.
Status: Unknown. Although it does not appear to be particularly numerous anywhere, it seems to be widespread and there have been many more sightings in recent years.

RISSO'S DOLPHIN

Grampus griseus

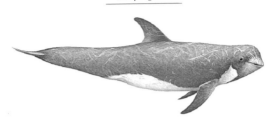

Risso's dolphins are unmistakable, with their slightly bulging foreheads, tall dorsal fins and distinctive battered appearance. The scratches and scars are mainly caused by the teeth of other Risso's dolphins, although confrontations with squid may also be to blame. Young animals are relatively unmarked.

Size: 2.6–3.8 m; 300–500 kg.
Distribution: Worldwide in deep tropical and warm temperate waters.
Diet: Squid seems to be the favourite prey, but also takes octopuses, fish and crustaceans.
Status: Hunted and caught in fishing nets in some countries, but still seems to be fairly common over much of its range.

IRRAWADDY DOLPHIN

Orcaella brevirostris

A rather unusual dolphin, resembling a small beluga (p.103) with a dorsal fin. In turbid conditions, it can be difficult to find but can sometimes be located by its loud blow. It has a strange habit of spitting water from its mouth while spyhopping.

Size: 2.1–2.6 m; 90–150 kg.
Distribution: Shallow coastal waters and major rivers of south-east Asia, from the Bay of Bengal to northern Australia.
Diet: Mainly fish, but also squid and crustaceans.
Status: The tropical river, estuarine and coastal habitat of this dolphin is very vulnerable to damming and other industrial development. Small-scale hunting and drownings in fishing nets affect sub-populations in some parts of the range, but it still appears to be locally common.

FRASER'S DOLPHIN

Lagenodelphis hosei

UNTIL the early 1970s, Fraser's dolphin had not been seen alive, but it is now regularly encountered on dolphin watching tours off the coast of St. Vincent, in the Caribbean, and elsewhere.

Size: 2–2.6 m; *c.*160–210 kg.
Distribution: Seems to be most common around the equator, especially in the Pacific, but also found in other deep tropical and warm temperate waters. Rarely seen inshore, except around oceanic islands and in areas with a narrow continental shelf.
Diet: Mainly mid-water fish, squid and crustaceans.
Status: Unknown numbers drown in fishing nets, and some are killed intentionally in Asia and elsewhere, but still appears to be fairly common at least in parts of its range.

BOTTLENOSE DOLPHIN

Tursiops truncatus

I N many ways,
the bottlenose dolphin is the
archetypal dolphin. Star of television programmes,
films and marine parks the world over, it is probably
the species most people imagine when the word
'dolphin' is mentioned. There are many varieties,
living in different parts of the world; some are almost

twice as long as others and they vary considerably in shape and colour. In a number of countries, wild bottlenose dolphins (usually males) become 'friendlies' and seem more interested in sharing the company of human swimmers and small boats than others of their own kind; they often remain in the same area for years.

Size: 1.9–3.9 m; 150–650 kg.
Distribution: Tropical, sub-tropical and temperate waters around the world, mainly close to shore but also far out to sea. Found in many enclosed seas, including the Gulf of California and the Red, Black and Mediterranean Seas.
Diet: Opportunistic feeders, with a wide range of feeding techniques. Will take fish, squid, crustaceans and a variety of other prey.
Status: Hunting in some areas, such as the Black Sea, appears to have reduced local populations; live captures for marine parks and zoos have also had a considerable impact in some areas. Unknown numbers are drowned in fishing nets. Otherwise, still seems to be fairly common over much of its range.

COMMERSON'S DOLPHIN

Cephalorhynchus commersonii

A striking animal, with a small, stocky body, this dolphin looks more like a porpoise. But it is very dolphin-like in its behaviour and is a fast and active swimmer, frequently riding the bow waves of passing boats and often swimming upside-down, spinning underwater as it goes.

Size: 1.3–1.7 m; 35–60 kg.

Distribution: Shallow coastal waters, with the main centre of distribution in southern Argentina, the extreme south of Chile around Tierra del Fuego, and the Falkland Islands. Also around Kerguelen Island in the Indian Ocean.

Diet: Fish, squid and crustaceans, taken mainly from near the bottom.

Status: Locally common, but hunting for use as crab bait in Chile and Argentina, and drownings in gill nets may be serious threats.

HECTOR'S DOLPHIN

Cephalorhynchus hectori

A distinctive little animal, with its 'Mickey Mouse-ear' dorsal fin, Hector's dolphin is a familiar sight in some parts of New Zealand. But its limited distribution and small surviving population give cause for concern and urgent action is needed to reduce the number of drownings in coastal gill nets.

Size: 1.2–1.5 m; 35–60 kg.
Distribution: Found only in New Zealand. Shallow coastal waters, mainly off South Island and the west coast of North Island.
Diet: Small fish and squid, may take crustaceans.
Status: Large numbers are drowned in coastal gill nets, and now an endangered species with a surviving population of some 3,000–4,000.

HEAVISIDE'S DOLPHIN
Cephalorhynchus heavisidii

JUST a few years ago, this striking dolphin was rarely seen and one of the least known of all cetaceans. Now there are regular tours to see them from Lambert's Bay, in South Africa.

Size: 1.6–1.7 m; 40–75 kg.
Distribution: Shallow, coastal waters of South Africa and Namibia. Normally within a few km of shore, it seems to be associated with the cold, northward-flowing Benguela Current.
Diet: Limited evidence suggests that this dolphin eats several varieties of fish and squid.
Status: Little is known about its status, although unknown numbers are drowned in coastal fishing nets and there is evidence of limited hunting in some areas.

BLACK DOLPHIN

Cephalorhynchus eutropia

THE black dolphin seems to be quite a shy animal, and is poorly known. One of the smallest of all cetaceans, it frequently enters estuaries and rivers. It appears all black at sea, but has a distinctive white belly and throat.

Size: 1.2–1.7 m; *c.*30–65 kg.
Distribution: Mainly cold, shallow, coastal waters of Chile, from the Straits of Magellan and the channels of Tierra del Fuego to about 30°S. Sometimes occurs at the extreme southern tip of Argentina.
Diet: Fish, squid and crustaceans.
Status: Hunted illegally for crab bait in southern Chile, and drowned in gill nets. The population is unknown, but it is believed to be small and declining.

HOURGLASS DOLPHIN

Lagenorhynchus cruciger

N AMED for the crude black and white hourglass pattern on its flanks, this species inhabits remote Antarctic and sub-Antarctic seas. However, it is frequently encountered by cruise ships on their way to the Antarctic Peninsula, and seems to enjoy riding in their bow waves and stern waves.

Size: *c*.1.6–1.8 m; 90–120 kg.
Distribution: High latitudes of the southern hemisphere, mainly between 45°S and 65°S, sometimes right up to the ice-edge. Mainly oceanic.
Diet: Believed to feed on small fish and squid.
Status: Never systematically exploited, the hourglass dolphin seems to be widespread and fairly common in many parts of its range.

PEALE'S DOLPHIN

Lagenorhynchus australis

PEALE'S dolphins tend to live in small groups and are found mainly in remote areas, so are seen relatively infrequently. However, they do sometimes ride the bow waves of large vessels and are known to swim alongside smaller ones. Striking animals close up, they have brilliant white 'armpits'.

Size: *c.*2–2.2 m; *c.*115 kg.

Distribution: Coastal waters of southern South America, especially around Tierra del Fuego and near kelp beds. Also seen regularly around the Falkland Islands. Frequently encountered in fjords, bays and inlets, but also over the continental shelf.

Diet: Relatively unknown, but believed to include a variety of fish and octopus.

Status: Locally common although, in the extreme south, there seems to have been a marked decrease in numbers where Peale's dolphins are harpooned for use as bait in crab traps.

ATLANTIC WHITE-SIDED DOLPHIN

Lagenorhynchus acutus

A T first glance, this species looks superficially similar to the common dolphin (p.136). But the position of the band on the tail stock, and the complex grey, white and black body patterning, make it quite a distinctive species at close range. It often feeds in association with fin, humpback and other large whales, and sometimes even rides their bow waves.

Size: 1.9–2.5 m; 165–200 kg.
Distribution: Cold temperate and sub-arctic waters of the northern North Atlantic, especially along the edge of the continental shelf.
Diet: Fish, including cod, herring and young mackerel, as well as squid and crustaceans.
Status: Despite a relatively small amount of exploitation, still seems to be abundant, especially in the western part of its range.

PACIFIC WHITE-SIDED DOLPHIN

Lagenorhynchus obliquidens

THESE dolphins are great fun to watch. They often live in large schools containing hundreds or even thousands of individuals and are so lively and boisterous that their splashes can be seen long before the animals themselves. They leap into the air and spin or turn complete somersaults before splashing back into the water, and often ride the bow waves of passing boats or ships.

Size: 1.7–2.4 m; 85–150 kg.
Distribution: Mainly offshore, or in very deep water closer to shore, in the northern North Pacific.
Diet: Anchovies, hake, pilchards and other fish, as well as small squid.
Status: Large numbers are killed in Japanese drive and harpoon fisheries, and in drift net fisheries elsewhere, but still fairly common over much of its range.

DUSKY DOLPHIN

Lagenorhynchus obscurus

THESE are social animals and frequently associate with a wide variety of whales and dolphins, as well as seals, a range of seabirds and even people. 'Duskies' are incredibly acrobatic, well known for their high leaps and somersaults.

Size: 1.6–2.1 m; 50–90 kg.

Distribution: Widely scattered in coastal, temperate waters throughout the southern hemisphere. Three main populations, in South America, southern Africa and New Zealand, as well as around Kerguelen and other offshore islands.

Diet: A wide variety of prey, in mid-water and near the bottom, including anchovies, lanternfish and squid.

Status: Relatively abundant throughout its range, although drowns in coastal gill nets and hunted in some areas.

WHITE-BEAKED DOLPHIN

Lagenorhynchus albirostris

DESPITE its name, the white-beaked dolphin does not always have a white beak. Although there are exceptions, individuals towards the west of the range tend to have dark or even black beaks. Strikingly large and robust for a dolphin, the white-beaked is capable of swimming at considerable speed and is frequently quite acrobatic.

Size: 2.5–2.8 m; 180–275 kg.
Distribution: Widely distributed in cool temperate and sub-Arctic waters of the North Atlantic, even at the edge of the polar ice.
Diet: Cod, herring, mackerel and a variety of other fish, as well as squid, octopus and crustaceans.
Status: Hunted in some areas, but still appears to be fairly common throughout much of its range.

YANGTZE RIVER DOLPHIN

Lipotes vexillifer

Nᴏ-ᴏɴᴇ knows exactly how many Yangtze river dolphins are left, but it is almost certainly the rarest cetacean in the world. There could be as few as a couple of dozen in the wild and there is just one, a single male called Qi-Qi, in captivity.

An estimated 12 per cent of the entire world human population lives in the river basin of the dolphin's home in the Yangtze River, China, so it faces an inordinate number of threats. Dangerous fishing hooks, overfishing, heavy boat traffic, pollution, riverbank development and dam construction contrive to ensure that it is already doomed in its natural home.

The last hope is to capture the few remaining survivors and transfer them to the relative safety of a semi-natural reserve. Against all the odds, on 19 December 1995, a female was captured near the central industrial city of Wuhan. Believed to be about 10 years old, she appeared to be fit and healthy and was released just after midnight into the waters of Shishou, a specially prepared semi-natural reserve. But in June 1996, just 6 months later, the female was dead. Meanwhile, another female has been found dead in the river. The project team is determined not to give up hope, but the future for the Yangtze river dolphin looks bleaker than ever.

Size: 1.4–2.5 m; 100–160 kg.
Distribution: Restricted mainly to the middle reaches of a 1,700 km stretch of the Yangtze River, in China.
Diet: Catfish and a large variety of other fish.
Status: Critically endangered. Many experts fear that it may be the first whale, dolphin or porpoise ever to become extinct as a direct result of human activity.

FRANCISCANA

Pontoporia blainvillei

DESPITE its classification as a river dolphin, this
species lives in the sea and is exceptional for
not entering freshwater. It is one of the smallest of
all cetaceans and yet has the longest beak (relative
to body size) of any dolphin.

Size: 1.3–1.7 m ; 30–53 kg.
Distribution: Temperate coastal waters of eastern
South America, mainly from the Doce River, in
Brazil, south to Bahía Blanca, in Argentina.
Although common in the La Plata estuary, and
some other estuaries, it rarely travels upriver.
Diet: Feeds mostly near the bottom, on a variety of
fish, squid and crustaceans.
Status: Locally common in parts of its range, though
may be threatened in some areas by incidental
catches in fishing nets.

AMAZON RIVER DOLPHIN

Inia geoffrensis

A strange-looking animal, with a pinkish body and enormous flippers, this dolphin tends to be more playful than its closest relatives. It has even been known to toss turtles into the air and grab fishermen's paddles. This is the largest and commonest of the river dolphins.

Size: 1.8–2.5 m; 85–160 kg.

Distribution: All the main rivers of the Amazon and Orinoco Basins, in Brazil, Colombia, Venezuela, Ecuador, Guyana, Peru and Bolivia. Occurs more than 3,000 km inland in some areas.

Diet: Wide variety of fish, especially bottom-living species.

Status: Vulnerable, although still fairly numerous in some areas. Facing a great many threats common to all river dolphins, as well as deforestation in its rainforest home.

INDUS RIVER DOLPHIN

Platanista minor

For many years, the Indus and Ganges river dolphins (opposite) were believed to be the same species. They look almost identical and have remarkably similar habits. However, recent research has revealed that they are quite distinct. Both species are endangered.

Size: 1.5–2.5 m; 70–90 kg.

Distribution: Turbid, silt-laden waters of the Indus River, in the Pakistani provinces of Sind and Punjab. More than 80 per cent of the population lives along a 170 km stretch in the lower reaches of the river.

Diet: Catfish and other fish, molluscs and crustaceans, probably caught near the bottom.

Status: Critically endangered. Threats include fishing, hunting, pollution and dam construction, and the population has already dropped to around 500.

GANGES RIVER DOLPHIN

Platanista gangetica

T HE Ganges and Indus river dolphins (opposite) are the only two cetaceans without a crystalline lens in their eyes. They can probably detect the direction – and perhaps intensity – of light, but for all intents and purposes they are blind. They find their way around and catch food by echolocation (see p.42).

Size: 1.5–2.5 m; 70–90 kg.
Distribution: Turbid, silt-laden waters of the Ganges, Meghna and Brahmaputra river systems of western India, Bangladesh, Nepal and Bhutan, and the Karnaphuli River, Bangladesh.
Diet: Mainly fish, molluscs and invertebrates.
Status: Endangered. Threats include fishing, hunting, pollution and dam construction. Estimated to be 4,000–6,000 left.

VAQUITA

Phocoena sinus

ONE of the rarest and most endangered cetaceans in the world. Even on official surveys in the northern Gulf of California, it often eludes professional biologists for days or even weeks at a time. Consequently, few people have ever seen the species alive and we know very little about its life and habits.

Size: 1.2–1.5 m; *c.*30–55 kg.
Distribution: Probably has the most restricted distribution of any marine cetacean. Found mainly within a 48 km radius in the extreme northern end of the Gulf of California (Sea of Cortez), in western Mexico.
Diet: Believed to feed on a variety of fish and, possibly, squid.
Status: Critically endangered. There are no more than a couple of hundred left. Several dozen are believed to drown in fishing nets every year.

HARBOUR PORPOISE

Phocoena phocoena

THE most widespread and commonly seen of all the porpoises. However, a brief glimpse of its dark back and low, triangular dorsal fin is all this undemonstrative little cetacean usually shows of itself. Its blow sounds like a human sneeze, giving it one of its alternative names, the puffing pig.

Size: 1.4–1.9 m; 55–65 kg.

Distribution: Cool temperate and sub-arctic coastal waters of the northern hemisphere.

Diet: Mainly schooling, non-spiny fish such as herring, whiting and mackerel, but also other fish, some squid and possibly crustaceans.

Status: Locally common within its range, but many thousands are drowned every year in gill nets, herring weirs and other fishing equipment. Still hunted in some areas. Its coastal habitat is probably to blame for high levels of pollutants found in the body tissues of harbour porpoises in many parts of the world.

BURMEISTER'S PORPOISE

Phocoena spinipinnis

E ASILY recognised by its small size and backward-pointing dorsal fin, but rather inconspicuous and rarely seen. It is believed to be considerably more abundant than the limited number of sightings would otherwise suggest, especially in the Strait of Magellan and Beagle Channel, around Tierra del Fuego.

Size: 1.4–2 m; *c.*40–70 kg.
Distribution: Shallow coastal waters of South America from Tierra del Fuego (the southernmost tip) north as far as northern Peru on the Pacific side and southern Brazil on the Atlantic side.
Diet: Believed to feed mainly on fish, but will also take a variety of squid and, possibly, crustaceans.
Status: Caught and drowned in gill nets, and has been heavily exploited for food in Peru and, to a lesser extent, Chile.

FINLESS PORPOISE

Neophocaena phocaenoides

ONE of the smallest of all cetaceans, this is the only porpoise without a dorsal fin. Instead of a fin on its back, it has a line of circular bumps, known as tubercles, which may be used by the females to 'carry' their calves. Despite two of its alternative names (see p.247) it is normally a pale blue-grey and only turns black after death.

Size: 1.2–1.9 m; 30–45 kg

Distribution: Warm, coastal waters and most major rivers of the Indo-Pacific. One of the best known populations lives in the Yangtze River, China.

Diet: Crustaceans, as well as small fish and squid.

Status: Locally common, although hunted for food in some parts of its range and caught and drowned in various gill net fisheries. Pollution and habitat destruction are likely to be serious threats in many areas near large human populations.

SPECTACLED PORPOISE

Australophocaena dioptrica

Named for the fine white line around each eye, this porpoise is rarely seen. Interestingly, the two sexes are quite different in appearance: the male has a large, rounded dorsal fin, while the female's is much smaller and more triangular in shape.

Size: 1.3–2.2 m; 60–84 kg.
Distribution: Mostly known from around the southern Atlantic coast of South America. However, there are also records from other widely separate locations across the southern hemisphere, including the Falklands, South Georgia, Kerguelen Islands, Heard Island, Macquarie Island and the Auckland Islands.
Diet: Believed to feed on a variety of fish and squid.
Status: May be locally common, but poorly known. In the past, at least, it has been killed deliberately for food and to be used as crab bait.

DALL'S PORPOISE

Phocoenoides dalli

DALL'S porpoise may be the fastest swimmer of all cetaceans. It produces a distinctive spray of water, called the 'rooster tail', which is produced by a cone of water coming off the animal's head as it rises to breathe. There are two distinct forms: the Dalli-type occurs throughout the range and has a smaller area of white on the flanks; and the Truei-type is found only in the western North Pacific and has more white.

Size: 1.7–2.2 m; 135–220 kg.
Distribution: Cold waters of the northern North Pacific, and adjacent seas. Often close to shore (usually near deep-water canyons) but also in the open sea.
Diet: Surface and mid-water fish and squid.
Status: Locally common within its range, although large numbers are killed by fisheries in the western North Pacific.

WHALE
WATCHING

HOW TO WATCH WHALES, DOLPHINS AND PORPOISES
Responsible whale watching

I T is sometimes easy to forget that we are uninvited guests in the world of whales, dolphins and porpoises. We have a responsibility to cause as little disturbance as possible – which is why whale watching should be an eyes-on, hands-off activity.

Fortunately, most whale-watch operators care about the whales, and their guests, and do a good job. They put the welfare of the animals before everything else, taking care not to disturb or injure them by manoeuvering their boats carefully, slowly and not too closely, and then leaving before the whales show signs of distress. A few operators, however, are not so careful and cause a great deal of unnecessary stress. Not only are the animals forced to steer clear of boats, or possibly even to abandon their preferred feeding or breeding grounds altogether, but collisions and other accidents can cause serious injury and even death.

The best trips also have knowledgeable naturalists on board to keep everyone well-informed; they provide free places for biologists to do urgently-needed research; and they help to raise money for whale conservation. They even play a valuable role in the local economy because, with a little planning and coordination, museums, science centres, bookshops, gift shops, bus companies, hotels and guesthouses, restaurants and cafés, taxi companies and many other businesses can all benefit from the tremendous influx of visitors coming to see the whales.

In this way, the best operators put something back for the whales. Educational trips help to drum up public support for their cause; the biologists learn more about their lives and needs; there is more money available to tackle important conservation issues; and the local people have good reason to look after the whales and their marine environment.

It is just up to individual whale watchers to choose the best and most responsible operators before booking their trips.

Humpback whale, New England, USA

Whale watching, Iceland

Clothing and equipment

T HE ideal choice of clothing and equipment obviously depends on where, when and how you intend to watch whales. But here are a few suggestions:

Binoculars

These are invaluable for finding whales, dolphins and porpoises, as well as for identifying them and studying their behaviour. Choose a magnification of 7–10x (anything higher will be unusable while you are bouncing around on a boat at sea).

Camera with zoom lens

An 80–200 mm lens (or a similar zoom) is ideal but, alternatively, a fixed lens of at least 135 mm can be useful for recording close encounters and interesting behaviour patterns. A motordrive is also useful. Do not forget to take plenty of film, and use a medium to fast speed (100–200 ASA depending on the weather and sea conditions).

Bottlenose dolphins, Ecuador

Hydrophone

Few whale watchers carry hydrophones (underwater microphones) because they are quite expensive and can be difficult to use. But they do help to find whales by sound, as well as adding a new and exciting dimension to the whale watching experience.

Identification guides

These are useful for identifying the whales, dolphins or porpoises you encounter. Consider taking guides to the birds, seals, fish and other local wildlife as well.

Notebook and pen

Use a small field notebook at sea (some people prefer a pocket-sized Dictaphone instead) and then copy your notes into a neat version later.

Polaroid sunglasses

These help to reduce the sun's glare and are excellent for seeing through reflections on the surface of the water. Attach them to a safety cord.

Rubber-soled deck shoes

These are important in case the deck gets wet with spray and becomes slippery.

Safety equipment

This should be provided on all organised whale watching trips. It might include lifejackets, life rafts, flares, a VHF radio, and first aid equipment.

Seasickness tablets or patches

These should be taken or applied in plenty of time before the trip.

Suntan lotion and sun hat
These are essential to avoid sunburn and sunstroke, especially around midday. Use a high factor lotion.

Telescope
A telescope (with tripod) can be useful when whale watching from shore, or from the relatively stable platform of a large cruise ship.

Warm and windproof clothing
This is vital if you are whale watching in cold weather. Remember that it is much colder at sea than it is on shore – so be careful not to under-estimate how many layers you are likely to need.

Waterproof bag
This is essential for protecting your spare clothing, binoculars, cameras and other equipment from salty air and spray.

Waterproof jacket and trousers
These are essential if sea conditions are likely to be rough or if you are expecting rain.

Whale watchers in survival suits, Canada

Finding the animals at sea

I N theory, it is possible to see whales, dolphins and porpoises almost anywhere in the world. They are found near the poles, at the equator, in freshwater rivers, along shallow coastlines, and even in the deep waters of the open sea.

But many species tend to be plentiful only in particular areas and, even then, are present only at certain times of the year. Their distribution also varies weekly, daily and hourly, according to many different factors such as sea and weather conditions, food availability and human disturbance. So even if you have done a little homework beforehand, and you are in roughly the right place at the right time, they can still be difficult to find.

People with a lot of experience at sea instinctively recognise the tiniest clues when they are looking for whales, dolphins and porpoises. They are trained to register the slightest movements and splashes that give their presence away.

With a large whale, for example, the first clue is often its blow or spout. This is more visible in some weather conditions than others, but it can be surprisingly distinctive. It may look like a flash of white (especially against a dark background) or a more gradual puff of smoke. Blows are easy to miss, though, especially since there is often a considerable gap between each one.

Alternatively, you may briefly see the head and back of the whale break the surface. This often resembles a strange wave that, somehow, does not look quite right. Anything suspicious, even if nine times out of ten it does turn out to be a wave, is worth investigating.

Splashes are also good clues. They can be caused by a large whale breaching, flipper-slapping or lobtailing – or by dolphins. A group of dolphins in the distance frequently looks like a rough patch of water, resembling lots of whitecaps and little breaking waves.

The presence of birds can often be a tell-tale sign as well, particularly if they seem to be feeding or are concentrated in one particular area. It makes sense that, if they have found a school of fish, there could be whales or dolphins feeding underneath.

Finally, do not forget to look *everywhere* – in front, behind, and to both sides. Scan the horizon with binoculars and use the naked eye to check nearer the boat (it is amazing how often people miss dolphins bow-riding right in front of them because they are too busy looking far out to sea). The golden rule is to be patient because, even in areas with well-known cetacean populations, it may take a while to track them down.

Feeding seabirds are often a tell-tale sign

Identification

I DENTIFYING whales, dolphins and porpoises at sea is a real challenge. In fact, it can be so difficult that even the world's experts are unable to identify every species they encounter: on most official surveys, at least some sightings have to be logged as 'unidentified'. But despite the inevitable frustrations, developing the necessary skills to tell one species from another can also be very satisfying.

There are several problems to deal with. The first, quite simply, is being on a boat: making detailed observations while trying to keep balance on a rolling, slippery deck can be difficult at the best of times. Adverse sea and weather conditions, such

Dusky dolphin, New Zealand

as a heavy swell, whitecaps, high winds, driving rain, or even glaring sunshine, add to the difficulties by making it almost impossible to get a good view and an accurate impression of the main features of the animal.

Then there are the whales, dolphins and porpoises themselves. They spend most of their lives underwater and, even when they come to the surface to breathe, frequently reveal little more than a brief glimpse of their dorsal fins and backs. Even a good view can be confusing, since many species look alike: it takes a highly trained eye to tell the difference between a pygmy sperm whale and a dwarf sperm whale, for example.

At the same time, individuals of the same species vary so much that they are rarely identical. Their dorsal fins are shaped differently, they show variations in their colouring, behave differently, and even come in a range of different sizes. Adult bottlenose dolphins, for example, vary in size from just under 2 m to nearly 4 m.

However, despite all these potential pitfalls, it is quite possible for anyone to recognise the relatively common and distinctive species and, eventually, many of the more unusual ones as well. It just requires some background knowledge and a little practice.

IDENTIFICATION CHECKLIST

The easiest way to identify whales, dolphins and porpoises is to use a relatively simple process of elimination. This involves running through a mental

checklist of fourteen key features every time a new
animal is encountered at sea. It is rarely possible to
use all fourteen features, and one alone is rarely
enough for a positive identification, but the best
approach is to gather information on as many as
possible before drawing any firm conclusions.

Geographical location

There is not a single place in the world where all 81
species of whales, dolphins and porpoises have been
recorded. In fact, there are not many places with
records of more than a few dozen species. This
immediately helps to cut down on the number of
possibilities. Atlantic white-sided dolphins, for
example, occur only in the North Atlantic, while
Pacific white-sided dolphins occur only in the North
Pacific.

Habitat

Just as cheetahs live on open plains rather than in
jungles, and snow leopards prefer mountains to
wetlands, most whales, dolphins and porpoises are
adapted to specific marine or freshwater habitats. For
example, Hector's dolphins are unlikely to be
encountered far out to sea, while sperm whales are
unlikely to be seen in shallow water.

Size

It is difficult to estimate size accurately at sea, unless a
direct comparison can be made with the length of the
boat or another object in the water. Therefore it is
better to use three simple categories: up to 3 m,
3–10 m, and over 10 m. In this way, simply by

deciding whether the animal is small, medium or large helps to eliminate a wide range of possibilities.

Unusual features

Some cetaceans have very unusual features, which can be used for a quick identification. These include the extraordinary curved teeth of the male strap-toothed whale, the long tusk of the male narwhal, and the callosities covering the heads of right whales.

Dorsal fin

The size, shape and position of the dorsal fin varies greatly between species. Some fins are tall and triangular, others are rounded, a few are little more than a hump, some have broad bases, others have narrow bases, some are curved, others are upright, and there is every possible combination in between; and, of course, a few species have no dorsal fin at all. The position of the fin on the animal's back is also a useful identification feature.

Flippers

The length, colour and shape of the flippers, as well as their position on the animal's body, vary greatly from one species to another. It is not always possible to see them, but flippers can be useful for identification in some species: in the humpback whale, for example, they are unmistakable.

Body shape

Much of the time, whales, dolphins and porpoises do not show enough of themselves to provide an overall impression of their shape. However, sometimes this can be a useful feature. For example, the vaquita has a noticeably robust body shape, while the finless porpoise is quite slender and streamlined.

Beak

The presence or absence of a prominent beak is a particularly useful identification feature in toothed whales. The Irrawaddy dolphin, for instance, has a rounded head without an obvious beak, whereas the long-snouted spinner dolphin has a very long, narrow beak.

Colour and markings

Many cetaceans are surprisingly colourful, and have distinctive markings such as body stripes or eye patches. Commerson's dolphins, for example, are markedly black and white, while Risso's dolphins are usually covered in white scratches and scars.

Risso's dolphin, Japan

Blue whale blowing, Mexico

Unfortunately, more subtle markings can be difficult to use for identification purposes, because colours at sea vary according to water clarity and light conditions. Also, bear in mind that the animal can appear much darker than normal if it is viewed against the sun.

Flukes

The flukes can be important features for identifying larger whales: some species lift their flukes high into the air before they dive, others do not. Minke and sei whales generally do not, for example, while humpbacks and sperm whales frequently do. It is also worth checking the shape of the flukes, looking for any distinctive markings and noticing whether or not there is a notch between the trailing edges.

Blow or spout

The blow is only really visible in larger whales. But it varies in height, shape and visibility between species and, especially on calm days, can be extremely useful for identification purposes. In fact, experienced observers can tell one species from another, even from a considerable distance, just by its shape. Right whales, for example, have wide, V-shaped blows, whereas fin whales produce single, narrow columns of spray.

Dive sequence

The dive sequence can be surprisingly distinctive in many species. Variations include: the angle at which the head breaks the surface; whether or not the dorsal fin and blowhole are visible at the same time; how strongly the tail stock is arched; the time interval between breaths; and the number of breaths before a deep dive.

DIVE SEQUENCES

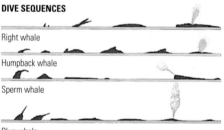

Right whale

Humpback whale

Sperm whale

Blue whale

Behaviour

Some species are more active at the surface than others, so any unusual behaviour can sometimes be useful for identification purposes. Among the large whales, for instance, humpbacks and right whales breach much more often than fin whales and blue whales.

Group size

Since some species are highly gregarious, while others tend to live alone or in small groups, it is worth noting the number of animals seen together. Beaked whales, for example, are normally seen alone or in small groups, whereas there could be dozens of long-finned pilot whales travelling together, or literally thousands of common dolphins.

THE GOLDEN RULE

It is often tempting to guess the identification of an unusual whale, dolphin or porpoise that you have not seen very clearly. But this is a mistake. Apart from the fact that it is bad science, it does little to improve your identification skills. Working hard at identification – and then enjoying the satisfaction of knowing that an animal has been identified correctly – is what makes a real expert in the long term.

It is perfectly acceptable to record simply 'unidentified dolphin' or 'unidentified whale', if a more accurate identification is not possible. But do write detailed notes for reference at a later date. As well as helping to improve your field skills, these notes may enable repeat sightings of species previously recorded as 'unidentified' to be turned into a positive identification days, weeks, months or even years later.

Recognising behaviour

WHALES, dolphins and porpoises are active animals and some of their more impressive and energetic displays take place in full view at the water surface. They slap the water with their flippers, fins or tails, ride in the bow waves of boats, lift their heads above the surface, and even leap high into the air and land back in the water with a tremendous splash.

We do not fully understand the meaning of many of these displays but, through research, we are beginning to unravel some of their secrets. Slapping the surface, for example, may be a form of courtship display, a way of signalling across great distances underwater, a technique for herding fish or dislodging parasites, a show of strength or a challenge ... or, in some cases, it could be simply for fun.

Breaching
When a whale launches itself into the air head-first, and falls back into the water with a splash, it is said to be breaching. Tail breaching is similar, but is tail-first instead of head-first and rarely lifts the whale as far out of the water.

Flipper-slapping
Many cetaceans lie on their sides or backs and slap one or both of their flippers onto the surface with a resounding splash. This is known as flipper-slapping, pectoral-slapping, pec-slapping or flipper-flopping.

Humpback whale breaching, SE Alaska, USA

Lobtailing

Lobtailing is an impressive display, especially in large whales, involving the forceful slapping of the flukes against the surface of the water. Also known as tail-slapping, it is done while the main body of the whale lies just under the surface.

Blowing or spouting

The blow or spout is the cloud of water droplets produced above a whale's head when it breathes out. It is also the term used to describe the act of breathing. In most small whales, dolphins and porpoises, the blow is low, brief and barely visible, but in large whales it can be very distinctive.

Fluking

When some large whales make a deep dive from the surface, they lift their tails high into the air to thrust their bodies into a more steeply-angled descent toward deeper waters. Bowheads, right whales, greys,

Bow-riding

blues, humpbacks and sperm whales all lift their flukes regularly, while a number of other species do from time to time.

Spyhopping
When whales and dolphins poke their heads above the surface of the water, apparently to have a look around, they are said to be spyhopping.

Bow-riding
Many dolphins, and some whales and porpoises, ride the bow waves of boats and ships, jostling for the best position where they can be pushed along in the water by the force of the wave. Some even ride the bow waves of large whales in exactly the same way. On some occasions they may simply be hitching a free ride but, when they actively go out of their way to ride in the bow waves, it is difficult to imagine that it can be anything more than exuberant play.

Wake-riding
Swimming in the frothy wake of a boat or ship seems to be a favourite pastime of many dolphins, and

some whales and porpoises. They surf, twist and turn in the waves, and even splash around and swim upside-down in the bubbles.

Logging

It is not uncommon to see groups of whales floating motionless at the surface together, usually all facing in the same direction. Known as logging, this is a form of rest.

Porpoising

When travelling at speed, many cetaceans literally leave the water each time they take a breath. Also known as running, this is believed to reduce friction on their bodies when they surface to breathe, which helps to conserve energy.

Fraser's dolphins porpoising, St. Vincent, Caribbean

Studying whales and dolphins

FOR years, the prospect of studying whales must have seemed about as difficult and challenging as exploring outer space. After all, these are animals that often live in extremely remote areas far out to sea, spend much of their lives diving to great depths underwater, and then show little of themselves when they rise to the surface to breathe. Many are quite shy and elusive, as well, and tend to avoid boats so, even at the surface, close encounters with them are almost impossible.

FROM EARLY BEGINNINGS TO HIGH-TECH RESEARCH

For a long time, the only information we had came from dead animals washed ashore, or killed by fishermen, and from the millions of whales slaughtered by commercial whalers. Then scientists began to study captive bottlenose dolphins and other small cetaceans in their concrete tanks.

But as we accumulated a wealth of data on basic whale biology, our knowledge of their lives under natural conditions, wild and free, was severely limited. In the days when modern technology had already taken us to the Moon and beyond, we were only just beginning to understand these extraordinary forms of intelligent life on our own planet.

The first attempts at wild whale research concentrated simply on counting whales – dead ones, initially, because they were so much easier to

count than live ones. It was not until the late 1960s
and early 1970s that a few pioneer biologists began
the painstaking process of counting live whales, and
then trying to learn more about their feeding
techniques, breeding habits, migrations and other
aspects of their daily lives.

Gradually, more and more people became
involved in whale research, and their information-
gathering techniques became increasingly
sophisticated. Modern whale researchers still study
whales in the traditional sense, simply watching
them through binoculars, for example. But, at the
same time, they frequently enlist the help of state-of-
the-art equipment and the kind of enterprising and
visionary research techniques that would make
NASA proud.

Satellites in space, deep-sea submersibles, radio
transmitters, high-tech directional hydrophones,
complex computer programmes, fibre optics, deep-
water video probes, DNA fingerprinting and, most
recently, the US Navy's Integrated Underwater
Surveillance System are now all part of the modern
whale researcher's armoury.

PHOTO-IDENTIFICATION

Biologists have been identifying individual animals
as part of their research for a long time. It is an
invaluable way of following their movements,
activities and associations over periods of days,
weeks, months and even years.

Whale and dolphin biologists identify individuals
in many different ways. Blue whales can be

Humpback whale showing the distinctive markings on the underside of its tail, New England, USA

recognised by the shape of the dorsal fin and the pattern of mottling on the body; individual humpback whales, on the other hand, are recognised by the unique black and white markings on the underside of the tail. The differences can often be quite subtle, so each animal is photographed to confirm its identity and to provide a permanent record of its existence. This technique is known as 'photo-identification', and has dramatically extended our knowledge of wild cetaceans in recent years.

DNA FINGERPRINTING

Do different calves with the same mother have the same father? Are individuals that spend a lot of time together related? These and many other intriguing questions can be answered just by examining a small

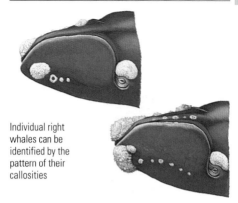

Individual right
whales can be
identified by the
pattern of their
callosities

piece of a whale's skin. More accurately, it is the
genetic material, or DNA, in the skin that is so
revealing. Just as one person's fingerprints are
different from everyone else's, no two animals have
exactly the same DNA – yet related animals show
some similarities. The clever detective work
involved in interpreting this information is called
'DNA fingerprinting', and it is already proving
invaluable in wild whale research.

RADIO- AND SATELLITE-TELEMETRY

It is possible to attach a specially-designed
transmitter to a whale or dolphin and then follow its
movements from a boat, a light aircraft or even a
research laboratory on the other side of the world.
Some transmitters are merely tracking devices, but

more sophisticated models can also provide information on the animal's swimming patterns, dive depths and heart rate, as well as environmental conditions, water temperature, and much more. There are basically two kinds of transmitter: radio transmitters, which send signals directly to receivers nearby, and satellite transmitters, which beam the signals up to orbiting communications satellites and from there back to receiving stations anywhere on Earth.

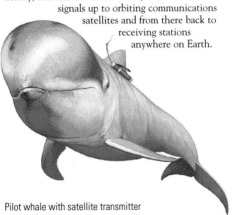

Pilot whale with satellite transmitter

EAVESDROPPING ON THE UNDERWATER WORLD

Whales, dolphins and porpoises live in a world that is dominated by sound, and a great deal can be learnt by listening to them underwater. This is such a challenging area of research that it has been likened to trying to find out what goes on in New York by dangling a microphone from the top of the Empire State Building. But experienced whale scientists, using sophisticated underwater microphones, called hydrophones, have been making some exciting discoveries in recent years.

A major development in this field came in 1992, when the US Navy opened its doors to the so-called Integrated Underwater Surveillance System. A series of sophisticated underwater listening stations on the seabed, originally designed for tracking enemy submarines, this offers some tremendously exciting possibilities for whale research in the future.

THE WHALE JIGSAW

There are still no short-cuts in whale research but, in recent years, the growth in our knowledge has been nothing short of remarkable. Studying such elusive creatures is like piecing together an enormously complicated jigsaw puzzle, where each piece of information brings with it new questions and unexpected surprises. The main difference, of course, is that the whale jigsaw will never be completely finished.

Nevertheless, it is encouraging to know that we have probably added more pieces in the past ten or twenty years than ever before.

WHERE TO WATCH WHALES, DOLPHINS AND PORPOISES
A world of whale watching

COMMERCIAL whale watching started in the mid-1950s, when people first began to take an interest in grey whales migrating up and down the coast of southern California. It is now a multi-million pound industry involving more than 65 countries and independent territories, from Argentina and Australia to Canada and Colombia.

It is possible to see most of the larger species, and many of the smaller ones, simply by purchasing a ticket and keeping your fingers crossed. Blues, humpbacks, fins, minkes, southern rights, northern rights, greys and many others are all there for the watching. It is even possible to choose *how* to watch them: from the air, from the shore, or from a host of different vessels, including yachts, rubber inflatables, motor cruisers, research boats, kayaks and huge ocean-going ships.

Every year, more than five million people join these organised whale watching trips, and many others venture out to sea on their own. Some are encountering whales for the first time, others are already addicted and spend every last bit of their spare time and money travelling around the world in search of new whale watching locations and new species.

They go to see family pods of killer whales in Canada, listen to singing humpback whales in

Hawaii, watch breeding southern right whales from
their hotel beds in South Africa, swim with dusky
dolphins in New Zealand, and enjoy many other
once-in-a-lifetime encounters with these enigmatic
creatures.

    This chapter describes some of the best-known
and most outstanding of the world's hot-spots for
whale watching. It is by no means a comprehensive
directory – that would fill many volumes – but it
describes more exciting whale-watch destinations
than anyone could ever hope to visit in a lifetime.
The places are numbered, and the numbers refer to
the map on pages 196–7.

Humpback whales, New England, USA

PLACES TO VISIT

The numbers refer to the places described on pages 198-240

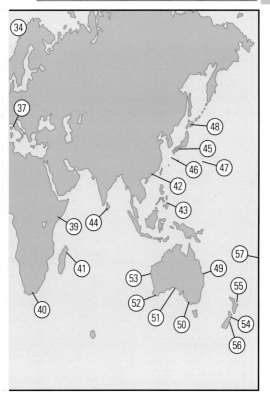

North America

Nᴏʀᴛʜ America is where commercial whale watching first began. Canada and the United States between them still attract more whale watchers than anywhere else in the world – and offer some of the best naturalist-led tours available.

A huge variety of cetaceans can be seen on boat trips from more than 120 communities on both the Atlantic and the Pacific coasts. In many cases, sightings are even guaranteed. There are some outstanding places to view whales from shore, as well, particularly in California and further north along the Pacific coast.

Humpback whale, New England, USA

UNITED STATES: NEW ENGLAND

More than a dozen towns in three New England states (Maine, Massachusetts and New Hampshire) offer whale watching in the Gulf of Maine (1). There are also whale-watch trips from New York and New Jersey. Humpbacks are the main attraction, but rare northern right whales, and fin, minke and pilot whales, Atlantic white-sided dolphins and harbour porpoises can be seen as well. The main season is May to early September, although there are often weekend-only trips in April and from mid-September until October.

Much of the action takes place over Stellwagen Bank and nearby Jeffreys Ledge, which are best described as underwater restaurants for whales. Every

Whale watching skipper, New England, USA

summer, huge numbers of whales gather over their shallow waters to gorge themselves on vast shoals of fish and crustaceans. In 1993, Stellwagen Bank was designated a US National Marine Sanctuary.

UNITED STATES: PACIFIC COAST

The variety of whales and whale watching opportunities is even greater on the Pacific coast than in New England.

Grey whales can be seen on boat trips and from shore for much of the year, either on migration or in summer residence. The ideal time depends on the location: in California (2), for example, the migration peaks in mid to late January; in Washington State, April and May are considered the best months. A few greys do not complete their full migration and spend the summer feeding off the coasts of Washington, Oregon and northern California.

Grey whale, California, USA

For land-based whale watching, there are hundreds of suitable vantage points all along the coast. Some are organised, such as Cabrillo National Monument with its glassed-in observatory and outdoor observation deck, but the majority are not. Some vantage points are better on the southward migration, others on the northward migration, so it is worth checking beforehand.

Many other cetaceans spend at least part of their year along the Pacific coast. Blue, humpback and killer whales are all in the area from June to October, for example, and there are Pacific white-sided dolphins, bottlenose dolphins, short-finned pilot whales, Dall's porpoises, harbour porpoises, and a variety of other species. Monterey submarine canyon, off central California, is particularly outstanding and has recorded no fewer than 26 different cetaceans, including some rare beaked whales. The best time for blues, humpbacks and other large whales in the Monterey area is August to October.

Killer whales can be seen around the San Juan Islands, in Washington State (3), during the summer. June and July are generally considered to be the best months. As well as regular boat trips, San Juan offers some wonderful opportunities to kayak with the whales.

HAWAII (4)

The main attraction in Hawaii is the humpback whales, which gather around the islands each year, from December until April, to mate and calve. Some areas have so many mothers and calves that they

Whale watching, Maui, Hawaii, USA

have been dubbed 'nurseries', and given special protection, while virtually the entire area is alive with the plaintive songs of the males.

For a long time, the only whale-watch tours were operated out of Lahaina, on the island of Maui. Even now, Lahaina's Front Street is one of the few places in the world where it is possible to go shopping for a whale-watch trip simply by wandering along the seafront.

Although the largest concentrations of humpbacks are west of Maui, the whales breed around all the islands. These days, there are whale watching trips from the Big Island of Hawaii, Oahu and Kauai as well.

SOUTH-EAST ALASKA (5)

South-east Alaska is the place to see humpback whales doing the unimaginable: fishing with nets made of bubbles (see p.81). Bubble-netting is all the more sensational because the climax of the action – hundreds of tonnes of gaping mouths simultaneously exploding out of the water – takes place above the surface and in full view of any whale watchers fortunate enough to be nearby.

As well as feeding humpbacks, there are pods of killer whales, minke and fin whales, Pacific white-sided dolphins, and Dall's and harbour porpoises. Even a few grey whales spend their summer in this spectacular, rugged region.

Whale-watch tours leave many different ports in south-east Alaska, including Gustavus, Juneau, Petersburg, Seward and Ketchikan, throughout the summer. There are a wide range of trips on offer: from kayaking to large-scale cruises and from day trips to two- or three-week wilderness excursions. There is even some super whale watching from several Alaska state ferries.

Humpback whale, SE Alaska, USA

WESTERN CANADA

There seem to be whales, dolphins and porpoises everywhere in western Canada: in bays, gulfs and sounds, close to shore, and farther out to sea.

There are migrating grey whales in March and April; killer whales and minkes in July, August and September (and, less frequently, in May, June and October); and small numbers of humpbacks and fin whales later in the year. Dall's porpoises, harbour porpoises and Pacific white-sided dolphins can also be seen.

Johnstone Strait (6), between the mainland and northern Vancouver Island, is one of the best places in the world to see killer whales. Trips leave from the little village of Telegraph Cove, and a number of other communities on Vancouver Island, and frequently encounter Dall's porpoises and other cetaceans as well. The best month – for weather, sea

Killer whale, Vancouver Island, Canada

conditions and whales – is normally August. The Queen Charlotte Islands also have killer whales, and a number of other species.

The best place to see grey whales is off the west coast of Vancouver Island, around the Pacific Rim National Park. Most tours leave from Tofino and Ucluelet.

EASTERN CANADA

There are four main areas for whale watching in eastern Canada: the St. Lawrence River, in central Quebec (7); the Gulf of St. Lawrence, in north-eastern Quebec (8); the Bay of Fundy, bordering Nova Scotia and New Brunswick (9); and Newfoundland (10). Between them, they offer blue, fin, humpback and minke whales, critically endangered northern right whales, belugas, long-finned pilot whales and several smaller cetaceans.

Canadian whale watching began in 1971, in the St. Lawrence River. Fin, humpback and minke whales can be seen on day trips from Tadoussac and neighbouring towns along the north side of the river, while boats from Les Escoumins and farther downstream have the best chance of seeing blues. This is also the southernmost place in the world to see belugas, which are usually encountered at the confluence of the saltwater St. Lawrence River and the freshwater Saguenay River. June to October are the best months, although the belugas (and some individuals of other species) are present year-round.

The Mingan Islands, in the Gulf of St Lawrence, are the home of Mingan Island Cetacean Study, a

Humpback whale, Newfoundland, Canada

research group which encourages whale watchers to observe and even take part in their work. The resident biologists specialise in blue whales, but also work with fin, minke and humpback whales, Atlantic white-sided and white-beaked dolphins, and harbour porpoises. Day tours as well as longer residential tours are available. The best months are from June until October.

In the Bay of Fundy, the highlight of any whale-watch trip is the northern right whale. The rarest large whale in the world, this species is teetering on the brink of extinction with fewer than 300 survivors in the North Atlantic. The Bay is a critically important feeding and nursery ground for northern right females and calves, from August to October, and is frequented by humpback, fin and

minke whales as well. It is accessible from south-west
Nova Scotia and eastern New Brunswick, but the
best starting point is Grand Manan Island.

Newfoundland is good for land-based whale
watching, with a number of excellent cliff tops to
look down directly onto the whales. But there are
also numerous boat tours to choose from, specialising
in humpback, fin and minke whales during the
summer, with long-finned pilot whales and various
other species turning up from time to time.

CENTRAL AND NORTHERN CANADA

Arctic whales are the speciality of central and
northern Canada. Belugas, narwhals and, with luck,
bowheads can all be seen in this region. The four
main locations are: Baffin Island (11), from May to
August, for all three species; Somerset Island, in
July, for beluga and narwhal; Inuvik, in the
Northwest Territories, in July and August, for
beluga; and Churchill, Manitoba (12), in July and
August, for beluga.

The most accessible of these is Churchill, on the
south-western shore of Hudson Bay. Better known as
the 'polar bear capital of the world', Churchill can
virtually guarantee belugas at the right time of year.
There are good half-day boat trips, but the whales
can even be seen from the outskirts of the town
itself. Unfortunately, polar bear numbers peak in late
October and early November, several months after
the belugas have left – but there are usually a few
bears around, and still some belugas, during late
August.

Latin America

I T is possible to join organised whale watching trips in many parts of Latin America, including Mexico, Belize, Colombia, Ecuador, Brazil, Chile and Argentina. Between them, they focus on a wide variety of species, from humpback and southern right whales to unusual small cetaceans such as Peale's and black dolphins.

There are also opportunities to see river dolphins in the Amazon and Orinoco rivers of eastern South America. The Amazon river dolphin and tucuxi can be seen fairly easily on many tropical rain forest excursions. Also the franciscana, or La Plata dolphin, is occasionally encountered on nature tours along the coasts of northern Argentina and Brazil.

PENÍNSULA VALDÉS (13)

Península Valdés, in Patagonia, Argentina, is internationally renowned for its southern right whales, which breed in two enormous bays on either side of the peninsula. They can easily be seen during the southern winter (mid-July to November) on day tours from the towns of Puerto Madryn, Trelew and Puerto Pirámides, or on longer package tours organised by international operators.

Punta Norte, on the tip of Península Valdés, is a regular hunting ground for several pods of killer whales. There is a special viewing area, overlooking a long stretch of beach, from which they can sometimes be seen stranding themselves to catch

Killer whale, Punta Norte, Argentina

young sea lions and elephant seals. It is an unforgettable sight, and the peak activity is usually in March.

BAJA CALIFORNIA

Every year, as many as 20,000 grey whales gather in their winter breeding grounds in Baja California (14). This long, desert peninsula on the Pacific coast of Mexico has been a popular whale watching destination since the early 1970s. It is particularly well known for its 'friendlies' – some of the animals will actually approach boats and allow tourists to touch them.

The grey whales tend to gather in three specific areas – Scammon's Lagoon, Magdalena Bay complex and San Ignacio Lagoon – and they are normally in the area from late December until April.

On the opposite side of Baja California is another outstanding whale watching area: a large stretch of water known as the Gulf of California, or Sea of Cortez (15). This is a wonderful region with blue, fin, Bryde's, humpback

Kayaking with a grey whale, Mexico

and sperm whales, common, bottlenose and Pacific white-sided dolphins, and numerous other species.

The best whale watching tours to the Sea of Cortez are on live-aboard boats from San Diego, California, or La Paz, Mexico. The best time is late December until April, and the tours typically last for one or two weeks.

COLOMBIA (16)

Colombia offers a variety of whale and dolphin watching opportunities: in the Amazon, for river dolphins and tucuxis, along the Caribbean coast for Bryde's whales, and along the Pacific coast for humpbacks. There are boat trips, as well as some good land-based viewing sites.

Most of the Pacific boats depart from Juanchaco, and take visitors to see a sizeable population of humpback whales just offshore. These whales migrate here from the Antarctic every year. They are in Colombia from August to October.

ECUADOR

Two of the best locations for whale watching in Ecuador (17) are Machalilla National Park, for boat trips from Puerto López and Salango, and the Hotel Punta Carnero, at Punta Carnero. The hotel affords a superb vantage point for land-based whale watching. In both locations, the main focus of attention from June to mid-September is the humpback whale, but dolphins and several other species can also be seen year-round.

There are many other whale and dolphin watching opportunities in Ecuador, not least around the Galapagos Islands (18), in an area that was declared a whale and dolphin sanctuary in 1990. Also, within a two-hour boat trip from the city of Guayaquil, as many as 500 bottlenose dolphins can be found in the Gulf of Guayaquil.

BRAZIL (19)

Brazil offers some outstanding whale and dolphin watching: humpback whales in Abrolhos National Marine Park, off southern Bahia State; southern right whales from the cliffs near the south end of Santa Catarina Island; tucuxis off the north coast of Santa Catarina Island; tucuxis and Amazon river dolphins in the rivers of the Amazon basin; and spinner dolphins at Fernando de Noronha archipelago, in Pernambuco State. There are also many other opportunities to see cetaceans up and down the country.

The Caribbean

T HE great appeal of whale watching in the Caribbean is the relaxed, warm setting and the crystal clear waters. More than half the 25 island countries and territories offer whale watching of one kind or another, and a third of all cetacean species spend part or all of their year in the region. Among them are pygmy and false killer whales, various beaked whales, dwarf and pygmy sperm whales, and a number of others that are rarely seen on whale watching trips in other parts of the world.

LESSER ANTILLES (20)

The relatively unspoilt island of Dominica was the first in the Caribbean to offer sperm whale watching. A resident group of about a dozen sperm whales lives off the west coast, and tours leave from near the town of Roseau. Pygmy sperm whales and dolphins are frequently seen on these trips, as well as occasional false killer whales, pilot whales and other species.

There is also dolphin watching from the island of St. Vincent. Fraser's dolphins are one of the main attractions for serious dolphin watchers, although spinner and spotted dolphins are seen more frequently; short-finned pilot whales are also encountered on many of the trips.

LITTLE BAHAMA BANK (21)

Little Bahama Bank, roughly between Grand Bahama Island and Florida, is an area less than about

Fraser's dolphins, St. Vincent, Caribbean

12 m deep where small groups of Atlantic spotted dolphins regularly swim with people who enter the water. There are few other places in the world where wild dolphins can be observed underwater with such consistency and in such superb, crystal clear conditions.

SILVER BANK (22)

The main breeding ground for humpback whales in the North Atlantic is an area of relatively shallow water called Silver Bank, which lies between the Dominican Republic and the Turks and Caicos Islands. Humpbacks also breed on other shallow banks in the Caribbean, but Silver Bank is where most whale watching takes place. From January to April, a handful of boats spend up to a week at a time on the Bank and, if conditions allow, encourage visitors to enter the water with the whales. It is one of the few places in the world where this is still allowed.

The best place for day trips to see humpback whales in the Caribbean is Samaná Bay, in the Dominican Republic.

BRITISH VIRGIN ISLANDS (23)

Tours from the north side of Tortola, in the British Virgin Islands, are almost unique in offering whale *listening* tours instead of whale *watching*. With the help of a hydrophone, and a good quality speaker system, humpback whale songs are played live in the boat – and the experience can be as moving and unforgettable as seeing the whales themselves.

Humpback whale, Dominican Republic

Europe

MORE than a dozen countries in Europe have some commercial whale watching, and the number continues to increase steadily. Although whale watching is fairly new and still developing in the region, many of the tours on offer are world-class, combining recreation, education, science, conservation and good business sense to provide a high quality service.

Europe is not as well known for its cetaceans as North America, New Zealand and some other parts of the world, but it has a surprising variety of species on offer. Blues, fins, minkes, humpbacks, killer whales, sperm whales and pilot whales are some of the larger species that can be seen, as well as an interesting variety of dolphins, and harbour porpoises. Europe also offers quality Arctic whale watching, which is less readily available in other parts of the world.

BRITAIN

Britain is home to a surprising variety of cetaceans, including minke, killer and long-finned pilot whales; Risso's, white-beaked, Atlantic white-sided and common dolphins; and harbour porpoises. Unfortunately, though, most of these live far out to sea and well away from urban areas, so Britain cannot offer the range of whale watching available in some other parts of Europe. The main attractions are minke whales and bottlenose dolphins.

There are three small, discrete populations of bottlenose dolphins: one of about 130 animals in the Moray Firth, east Scotland (24); a second, believed to be roughly the same size, in Cardigan Bay, west Wales (25); and a third of about 55 animals living around the coasts of Dorset, Devon and Cornwall (26). The Moray Firth is where the most popular tours are currently centred and, indeed, is one of the best sites for boat- and shore-based dolphin-watching in Europe. Day trips also leave from New Quay, in Dyfed, to see the Welsh population of bottlenose dolphins and a variety of other wildlife almost year-round (weather permitting).

Minke whales are most frequently seen in northern and western Scotland, although they are sometimes encountered in other areas as well. There are regular tours to see them during the summer from the Isle of Mull (27), in addition to Gairloch and various ports in the Moray Firth area.

Whale watching, Isle of Mull, Scotland

IRELAND

Ireland offers some of the best land-based whale watching in Europe. Several of the better vantage points, in the south-west, boast sightings of no fewer than twelve different species. There are also boat trips in this corner of Ireland, specialising in whale and bird watching around Mizen Head, Cape Clear (28) and Fastnet Rock. The cetaceans seen can include minke and pilot whales, harbour porpoises, and bottlenose, common and Risso's dolphins.

A resident group of bottlenose dolphins in the mouth of the Shannon Estuary (29), in western Ireland, can be seen year-round (weather permitting) on boat trips from Carrigaholt.

Dingle Harbour, County Kerry (30), also deserves a special mention. This is the home of Fungie, a solitary bottlenose dolphin that has entertained more than a million visitors since he turned up unexpectedly in the mid-1980s. Nowhere else in the world can claim a multi-million-pound-a-year industry based on a single dolphin.

GREENLAND (31)

Greenland is beginning to make a name for itself as a superb destination for Arctic whales, while its dramatic, icy setting makes watching other whale species especially memorable.

Narwhals and belugas are frequently encountered off the west coast, particularly north of Disko Bay, as well as fin and minke whales, occasional sperm whales, killer whales and various dolphins. The south-west coast is notable for its humpback whales, which gather in this relatively warm corner of the country to feed throughout the summer.

ICELAND (32)

Whale watching is relatively new to Iceland – the first commercial trip was in 1991 – but there are already more than a dozen operators working from almost as many different towns and villages all around the coast. Currently, Iceland has the fastest growing whale-watch industry in Europe.

The sheer variety of species being seen is also quite remarkable. Minke, humpback and fin whales are regularly encountered inshore, as are killer whales, harbour porpoises, and Atlantic white-sided and white-beaked dolphins. The minke whales, in particular, frequently associate with whale watching boats and provide outstanding photo opportunities.

Whale watching, Iceland

Blue whales occasionally come inshore as well and, together with sperm whales, are regularly encountered a little farther offshore.

In addition to this impressive list of cetaceans, Iceland also offers the midnight sun, spectacular seabird colonies, and some of the most breathtaking scenery on Earth. It is not surprising that the 'Land of Fire and Ice' is becoming such a popular destination for whale watchers from all over the world.

THE FAROE ISLANDS (33)

The Faroes lie halfway between Scotland and Iceland, in the north-east Atlantic, and are probably better known for killing whales than watching them. Long-finned pilot whales have been hunted around the islands for hundreds of years (see p.57) and, consequently, many foreigners are unwilling to visit the islands on moral grounds.

However, it is possible to see the pilot whales, as well as Atlantic white-sided and white-beaked dolphins, during more general nature and bird-watching tours. Killer whales, minke whales and even sperm whales all occur in the area, while the rare, deep-diving northern bottlenose whale is present in smaller numbers.

NORWAY (34)

The fishing port of Andenes, in northern Norway, is one of the best places to see sperm whales. Tours are led by Whale Safari Ltd, which is one of the finest whale-watch operators in the world. Male sperm

whales gather to feed in deep waters beyond the
continental shelf, only two or three hours away by
boat, and are encountered on almost every trip. Fin
and minke whales, long-finned pilot whales, killer
whales, harbour porpoises and white-beaked
dolphins are also sometimes seen. As a special
bonus, there are daily slide shows and lectures, and a
wide range of exhibits on whale biology and
whaling, in a newly-built information centre.

The other hot-spot for whale watching in
Norway is the Tysfjord area, a little further south.
Every autumn, literally hundreds of killer whales
arrive to feed on herring, and the sight of the large,
carefully-coordinated pods corralling the fish is
unforgettable. Unfortunately, the whale-watching
season is restricted to a six-week period before the
end of November, and is limited by only 4–6 hours
of daylight each day; the whales stay for the winter
but, after November, there is too little daylight to
watch them.

Whale watching, Tysfjord, northern Norway

THE CANARY ISLANDS (35)

Every year, more than half a million people go whale watching from the island of Tenerife, in the Canary Islands. It has become the second most popular place in the world to watch whales, after New England, USA.

Short-finned pilot whales, Tenerife, Canary Islands

Despite being a tourist hot-spot, Tenerife is probably the best location in the world to see family groups of short-finned pilot whales. There are about 500 of these large members of the dolphin family living close to shore year-round, and they are easily found on half-day trips from Playa de las Americas, Los Cristianos and other resorts along the south coast. There are also bottlenose dolphins in the area, as well as several predominantly tropical dolphins. A wide variety of other species, from sperm whales to beaked whales, are seen from time to time, especially around the nearby island of Gomera.

More recently, whale and dolphin watching tours have started to operate from Gran Canaria and Lanzarote as well.

THE AZORES (36)

The Azores is a well-kept secret. It is not particularly well known as a whale watching destination, yet offers some of the best whale watching in the world. It is a delightful archipelago, belonging to Portugal but lying some 1,400–1,800 km far out in the Atlantic, and is home to an astonishing variety of whale and dolphin species.

Sperm whales are the main focus of attention. Unlike the male-only populations off the coasts of Norway and New Zealand, the whales here are mainly females and their young. Short-finned pilot whales, as well as bottlenose, common, Risso's, spotted and striped dolphins, are also seen regularly. But the exciting bonus is that many other species turn up from time to time, including blue whales,

humpbacks, false killer whales and, in particular,
several different beaked whales. Most of the whale
watching is centred around the islands of Pico and
Faial, and takes place mainly from May to October.

There is also good land-based whale watching in
the Azores. The vigias, or watch towers, originally
used by whalers, are now being restored and opened
to the public. They are manned by experienced
whale watchers, who help guide the boats at sea to
find the whales.

THE MEDITERRANEAN

The Mediterranean is home to a wonderful variety
of whales and dolphins, although there are relatively
few whale-watch operators in the region. Bottlenose,
common and striped dolphins are frequently seen,
together with fin whales in certain areas, and it is
also possible to see sperm whales, pilot whales and
Risso's dolphins. With a great deal of luck, even the
rare Cuvier's beaked whale is sometimes
encountered.

The greatest potential probably lies in the
Ligurian Sea (37), which is the most reliable area to
see fin whales in the Mediterranean. There are
departures from Toulon, Nice and other places in
southern France; Monaco; and San Remo and
Imperia in Italy.

GIBRALTAR (38)

Europe's first commercial whale-watch trips took
place in Gibraltar, in 1980, when an ex-fisherman
began to take people to see the local dolphins.

Common dolphin, Gibraltar

These days, more than 10,000 people join several different operators to watch bottlenose, common and striped dolphins close to the shore every year. All three species are fairly common in the Bay of Gibraltar year-round, while killer whales sometimes appear in May and June, and several other species occur from time to time. Sperm whales and others are known to occur in the Straits of Gibraltar, but not often enough to support commercial whale watching.

Africa

THERE is organised whale and dolphin watching in a number of different countries in Africa, including Egypt, the Gambia, Mauritania, Kenya (39) and, in particular, South Africa and Madagascar. Several species of whales and dolphins live along the coastline of other countries on the continent but, as yet, there are no organised tours.

SOUTH AFRICA (40)

In South Africa, there is really no need to get out of bed in the morning to watch whales. Between July and late October every year, southern right whales come so close to shore that it is possible to watch them from hotel rooms, as well as cafés, restaurants and anywhere else within viewing distance of the sea.

There is even a 'Whale Route' – a meandering scenic road which starts in Cape Town and twists and turns its way to the southernmost tip of the continent and beyond – with dozens of lookouts for pulling off the road to watch the whales.

The heart of the Whale Route is a town called Hermanus, where the locals virtually have whales in their back gardens: they can watch as many as a couple of dozen of them cavorting in the bay from their lounges, kitchen sinks or bedrooms. Hermanus is also home to the world's first whale crier, who strolls around town blowing a bass kelp horn to alert locals and visitors to the most recent whale sightings.

South Africa has some of the strictest whale protection laws in the world and, consequently, there are no boat tours to view the southern right whales (although there are boat tours to see Heaviside's dolphins from Lambert's Bay, as well as Bryde's and humpback whales in other parts of the country). This may change in the future, since the regulations are currently being reviewed, but in the meantime South Africa offers some of the best land-based whale watching in the world.

MADAGASCAR

The main focus of whale watching in Madagascar is the east coast. From July until September every year, large numbers of humpback whales gather in the area between the island of Sainte-Marie (Nosy Boraha) and Baie d'Antongil, around the Masoala Peninsula (41), to mate and raise their young. Most of the whale watching tours leave from Sainte-Marie Island.

There are more humpbacks in other parts of Madagascar, as well as fin whales and bottlenose, spinner and Indo-Pacific hump-backed dolphins; sperm whales can be found farther offshore.

Whale watcher, Hermanus, South Africa

Asia

A SIA is a vast and varied region with plenty of whale and dolphin watching opportunities, but relatively few organised tours. However, the number of operators has grown steadily in recent years and more are likely to start whale watching in the not-too-distant future. At least a dozen countries already offer tours of one kind or another, and it is possible to see anything from spinner dolphins in Bali and rare arctic whales in Russia to finless porpoises in China and even Ganges river dolphins in Nepal.

HONG KONG (42)

Hong Kong is one of the least likely places for dolphin watching. But since the first trips began there, in 1994, it has steadily grown in popularity.

The local speciality is the 'pink dolphin', or 'Chinese white dolphin', which is actually a unique form of the Indo-Pacific hump-backed dolphin. It gets its local name from the skin, which is mottled grey-white initially but then takes on a pinkish hue as the animal matures. There is no easier place in the world to see Indo-Pacific hump-backed dolphins, which occur in Hong Kong year-round.

There could be as many as 200 Indo-Pacific hump-backed dolphins in Hong Kong and the neighbouring Zhu Jiang (Pearl River) delta. They are most often encountered in the shadow of the new Hong Kong airport; but this is causing massive changes to their favoured haunts and, in the future, may affect both the dolphin population and the opportunities for watching them.

PHILIPPINES

A wide variety of tropical whales and dolphins can be seen around the numerous islands of the Philippines. Organised, boat-based whale watching is available in Tanon Strait (43), where some of the highlights include Fraser's dolphins, melon-headed whales and dwarf sperm whales, which are normally difficult to see anywhere else in the world.

SRI LANKA (44)

In the early 1980s, a small population of blue whales was discovered living off the north-east coast of Sri Lanka, near a town called Trincomalee. It was an exciting find and, almost immediately, local

Whale watching, Trincomalee, Sri Lanka

conservationists began taking people out to see them.

Unfortunately, simmering strife between the Sinhalese people and Tamil separatists exploded at about the same time, and the country was plunged into a state of civil war. The troubles continue to this day and, although two-thirds of the island is largely unaffected, Trincomalee is in the troubled one-third and has suffered intense fighting and guerrilla activity for many years.

Meanwhile, the whale watching has been put on hold. But once the war is over, Trincomalee is likely to become a major hot-spot for whale watchers from all over the world. As well as the blue whales (which can even be seen from lookouts on shore) there are sperm and Bryde's whales and a variety of tropical dolphins.

JAPAN

Whale watching in Japan? Not many years ago, it would have seemed about as likely as scuba diving in Nepal, downhill skiing in Holland, or beach holidays in Spitzbergen. After all, the only whales the Japanese are supposed to like are dead ones, cut up into bite-sized pieces and served as whale sukiyaki or raw whale sashimi.

But Japan has one of the fastest-growing whale-watch industries in the world. Despite a relatively late start, in the 1980s, it has already grown to involve more than 20 towns and villages up and down the country – and attracts no fewer than 60,000 people every year. Even more interesting is the fact that most of the whale watchers are Japanese.

Whale watching, Cape Muroto, Japan

In one way, Japan is an obvious candidate for whale watching, because it has so many interesting species close to shore. For example, Ogata and several other towns and villages in Kochi prefecture, on Shikoku Island (45), offer some of the best Bryde's whale watching in the world. The whales live within sight of shore and are seen most frequently between March and October. Further south, the tropical islands of Okinawa (46) and Zamami, and the Ogasawara group (47), are important breeding grounds for humpback whales; they are present during the winter and the best time to see them is from February to April. At the other end of the country, general nature tours leave from a number of towns and villages on the northern island of Hokkaido (48), and promise frequent sightings of minke whales, Pacific white-sided dolphins and Dall's porpoises from March until October.

One of the most famous whale-watch locations in Japan is Cape Muroto, a wild and rugged finger of land on Shikoku, in the south-west. The operator is an ex-whaler who spent nearly half his life killing whales and, as a harpooner, actually won awards for some of the largest catches on record. But in the late 1980s he had a change of heart and, ever since, has been taking tourists to see sperm whales, short-finned pilot whales, Risso's dolphins, bottlenose dolphins and a varied selection of other species living virtually within sight and sound of his home town.

Australasia and the South Pacific

AUSTRALIA, New Zealand and Tonga have a wide range of whale and dolphin watching opportunities: from the shore, from the air, from boats, and even for snorkellers in the water. The main large whale species are humpbacks, southern rights and sperm whales, but many others are encountered from time to time, as well as a great variety of dolphins.

AUSTRALIA

There are whale watching opportunities at strategic locations around much of the Australian coastline. These tend to focus on humpbacks and southern right whales, both of which are readily found inshore at the right times of year, although Bryde's and sperm whales, and a variety of others, may be encountered as well. There are also a number of dolphin watching operations and, indeed, the most famous land-based dolphin watching site in the world.

Australia's boat-based whale watching began in 1987, in Hervey Bay, Queensland (49). The most commonly watched species in Queensland is the humpback whale, which is seen on migration, as well as on its breeding grounds in the Whitsundays and other areas of the north, in the lee of the Great Barrier Reef. The season in the Whitsundays is July until September, in Hervey Bay from the middle of August until late October.

Humpback whales are also the focus of whale-watch trips in New South Wales, on their migratory route along the east coast of Australia. Depending on the latitude, the season begins as early as late June (Coff's Harbour) and continues until the beginning of December (Eden, Merimbula, and others). Occasional sightings of southern right, blue, minke, Bryde's, sperm and killer whales have been reported in most NSW whale-watch areas as well.

The whale watching in Victoria is mainly land-based. In particular, southern right whales can be seen from May until October on their breeding grounds at Logan's Beach, near Warrnambool (50), where they come close to shore. There are special observation platforms on high dunes above the beach.

Bottlenose dolphin in Monkey Mia, Western Australia

The southern right whale is the most commonly encountered whale in the sheltered coastal bays and inlets of South Australia. Again, the whale watching in this part of the country is mainly land-based, in areas such as Nullarbor (51) and Victor Harbour, and lasts from mid-June until late October.

In Western Australia, from July through to late November, depending on the latitude, whale-watch trips take people to see humpback whales. Southern right whales can also be seen from August until November around Albany (52), site of Australia's last whaling station.

Wild bottlenose dolphins have been greeting people in the shallows at Monkey Mia, in Shark Bay, Western Australia (53), for more than three decades. Several times a day, most often from April to October, half a dozen or more dolphins make the pilgrimage to Monkey Mia beach. They swim between people's legs, wait to be scratched and tickled, and play catch with pieces of seaweed or fish. Sometimes, they beach themselves in no more than a few centimetres of water, and simply watch the crowds gathered to see them. Monkey Mia is a long way from anywhere – Perth, the nearest city, is 765 km away – but it is worth the effort.

New Zealand

The whale watching capital of New Zealand is Kaikoura, on the east coast of South Island (54). Sandwiched between the sea and a spectacular range of snow-capped mountains, it is one of the best places in the world to see sperm whales close to

Sperm whale, Kaikoura, New Zealand

shore. The whales are year-round residents, living
literally within sight of the town, and can be seen on
whale-watch trips run by the local Maori people.
There are also tours to watch the whales from the
air, by helicopter or seaplane.

Migratory humpback whales pass through the
area in June and July, and killer whales are seen
quite often during the southern summer. Kaikoura
also has trips to watch and swim with large,
boisterous schools of dusky dolphins, which move in
close to shore from October until April, and
Hector's dolphins, which are found only in New
Zealand and occur year-round. Not surprisingly, the
number of tourists visiting Kaikoura has increased
30-fold in the past decade and, today, the town
attracts more than 100,000 whale and dolphin
watchers every year. Booking ahead is essential.

There are many other whale and dolphin

watching opportunities in New Zealand. Hot-spots include the Bay of Islands (55), Tauranga and Whakatane, on North Island; and Banks Peninsula (56), Picton, Te Anau and Marlborough Sound, on South Island. As well as dusky and Hector's dolphins, bottlenose dolphins, common dolphins and a number of other species can be seen.

TONGA

The tropical islands of Vava'u, in Tonga (57), lie in the heart of an important breeding ground for humpback whales. During the southern winter, from July to November, the whales gather in the waters around this picturesque South Pacific archipelago to mate and calve. With the help of a sophisticated hydrophone, the hauntingly beautiful songs of the males are relayed through speakers on board the whale-watch boat and, if conditions are suitable, participants are allowed to get in the water and snorkel with the whales. Spinner dolphins and pilot whales are also seen on some of the trips.

Dusky dolphins, Kaikoura, New Zealand

Antarctica

ANTARCTICA is the ultimate whale-watch destination. It is an expensive place to visit (the only way to get there as a tourist is aboard a cruise ship) but it offers more whales and dolphins than most people will ever see anywhere else in the world. With huge numbers of penguins, seals and other wildlife as well, and a spectacular icy setting, it is the trip of a lifetime.

Most Antarctic cruises leave from the southern tip of South America (normally Ushuaia, in Argentina, or Punta Arenas, in Chile) and pass through several different marine habitats in the space of two or three weeks. The inshore waters of Tierra del Fuego (and South Georgia (58) and the Falklands (59), if they are included in the itinerary);

Humpback whales, Antarctica

the high seas of the Drake Passage, and the region of broken ice around the Antarctic Peninsula itself (60) each have their own cetacean specialities.

Baleen whales migrate to Antarctic waters every summer to spend several months feeding on crustaceans. Humpback, fin, sei, minke and even southern right and blue whales can be seen during an Antarctic cruise. Toothed whales which may be seen include sperm whales, long-finned pilot whales, southern bottlenose whales and various members of the beaked whale family. Orcas or killer whales, and hourglass, Commerson's, Peale's and southern rightwhale dolphins are all frequently encountered as well. Even this is not an exhaustive list, since many other species are identified from time to time.

Despite such fabulous whale watching opportunities, the number of whales surviving in Antarctica today is small compared with the number there at the turn of the century. This is when the whaling industry began more than 60 years of slaughter in the Southern Ocean. Even now, some 30 years after the worst of the whaling stopped, blue whales are struggling on the verge of extinction and most of the other large whales still exist in far fewer numbers.

The Southern Ocean Whale Sanctuary, which was approved in 1994 and covers an area of some 50 million square kilometres around the entire continent of Antarctica, provides some hope for the future. Unfortunately, though, Japan does not accept the protection of minke whales, and continues to hunt this species in the sanctuary.

FURTHER READING

Carwardine, Mark, *Eyewitness Handbooks: Whales, Dolphins and Porpoises*, Dorling Kindersley, London, 1995.

Carwardine, Mark, *The Book of Dolphins*, Dragon's World, London, 1996.

Darling, James D., Nicklin, Charles 'Flip', Norris, Kenneth S., Whitehead, Hal and Würsig, Bernd, *Whales, Dolphins and Porpoises*, National Geographic Society, Washington, 1995.

Hoyt, Erich, *Riding with the Dolphins - The Equinox Guide to Dolphins and Porpoises*, Camden House, Ontario, 1992.

Hoyt, Erich, *Meeting the Whales - The Equinox Guide to Giants of the Deep*, Camden House, 1991.

Leatherwood, Stephen, and Reeves, Randall R., *The Sierra Club Handbook of Whales and Dolphins*, Sierra Club Books, San Francisco, 1983.

Martin, Anthony R., *Whales and Dolphins*, Salamander Books, London, 1990.

Species Checklist
Baleen whales

FAMILY: ESCHRICHTIIDAE
1. Grey whale (*Eschrichtius robustus*) (p. 68)
Other names: California grey whale, mussel-digger, devilfish, scrag whale

FAMILY: BALAENIDAE
2. Bowhead whale (*Balaena mysticetus*) (p. 72)
Other names: Greenland right whale, Greenland whale, Arctic right whale, Arctic whale, great polar whale
3. Northern right whale (*Eubalaena glacialis*) (p. 74)
Other names: black right whale, Biscayan right whale
4. Southern right whale (*Eubalaena australis*) (p. 74)

FAMILY: NEOBALAENIDAE
5. Pygmy right whale (*Caperea marginata*) (p. 77)

FAMILY: BALAENOPTERIDAE
6. Humpback whale (*Megaptera novaeangliae*) (p. 78)
Other names: hump-backed whale
7. Minke whale (*Balaenoptera acutorostrata*) (p. 86)
Other names: finner, little finner, sharp-headed finner, pike whale, little piked whale, pikehead, lesser finback, lesser rorqual
8. Bryde's whale (*Balaenoptera edeni*) (p. 88)
Other names: tropical whale
9. Sei whale (*Balaenoptera borealis*) (p. 90)
Other names: sardine whale, pollack whale, coalfish whale, Japan finner, Rudolphi's rorqual
10. Fin whale (*Balaenoptera physalus*) (p. 92)
Other names: finback, finner, herring whale, common rorqual, razorback
11. Blue whale (*Balaenoptera musculus*) (p. 94)
Other names: sulphur-bottom, Sibbald's rorqual, great northern rorqual

Toothed whales

FAMILY: PHYSETERIDAE
12. Sperm whale (*Physeter macrocephalus*) (p. 96)
Other names: cachalot, great sperm whale

FAMILY: KOGIIDAE
13. Pygmy sperm whale (*Kogia breviceps*) (p. 100)
Other names: lesser sperm whale, short-headed sperm whale, lesser cachalot
14. Dwarf sperm whale (*Kogia simus*) (p. 100)
Other names: Owen's pygmy sperm whale

FAMILY: MONODONTIDAE
15. Narwhal (*Monodon monoceros*) (p. 102)
Other names: narwhale
16. Beluga (*Delphinapterus leucas*) (p. 103)
Other names: belukha, sea canary, white whale

FAMILY: ZIPHIIDAE
17. Arnoux's beaked whale (*Berardius arnuxii*) (p. 105)
Other names: southern beaked whale, southern four-toothed whale, southern giant bottlenose whale, New Zealand beaked whale
18. Baird's beaked whale (*Berardius bairdii*) (p. 105)
Other names: northern giant bottlenose whale, giant four-toothed whale, northern four-toothed whale, North Pacific bottlenose whale, North Pacific four-toothed whale
19. Northern bottlenose whale (*Hyperoodon ampullatus*) (p. 106)
Other names: North Atlantic bottlenosed whale, flathead, bottlehead, steephead
20. Southern bottlenose whale (*Hyperoodon planifrons*) (p. 107)
Other names: Antarctic bottlenosed whale, flathead
21. Sowerby's beaked whale (*Mesoplodon bidens*) (p. 107)
Other names: North Sea beaked whale
22. Andrew's beaked whale (*Mesoplodon bowdoini*) (p. 108)
Other names: Bowdoin's beaked whale, splay-toothed beaked whale, deepcrest beaked whale

23. Hubb's beaked whale (*Mesoplodon carlhubbsi*) (p. 109)
Other names: arch-beaked whale
24. Blainville's beaked whale (*Mesoplodon densirostris*) (p. 109)
Other names: tropical beaked whale, dense-beaked whale, Atlantic beaked whale
25. Gervais' beaked whale (*Mesoplodon europaeus*) (p. 110)
Other names: Gulf Stream beaked whale, European beaked whale, Antillean beaked whale
26. Ginkgo-toothed beaked whale (*Mesoplodon ginkgodens*) (p. 111)
Other names: ginkgo beaked whale, Japanese beaked whale
27. Gray's beaked whale (*Mesoplodon grayi*) (p. 111)
Other names: scamperdown whale, southern beaked whale
28. Hector's beaked whale (*Mesoplodon hectori*) (p. 112)
Other names: New Zealand beaked whale, skew-beaked whale
29. Strap-toothed whale (*Mesoplodon layardii*) (p. 113)
Other names: strap-tooth beaked whale, Layard's beaked whale
30. True's beaked whale (*Mesoplodon mirus*) (p. 113)
Other names: wonderful beaked whale
31. Stejneger's beaked whale (*Mesoplodon stejnegeri*) (p. 114)
Other names: Bering Sea beaked whale, North Pacific beaked whale, sabre-toothed beaked whale
32. Lesser beaked whale (*Mesoplodon peruvianus*) (p.115)
Other names: Peruvian beaked whale, pygmy beaked whale
33. Longman's beaked whale (*Mesoplodon pacificus*) (p. 115)
Other names: Pacific beaked whale, Indo-Pacific beaked whale
35. Bahamonde's beaked whale (*Mesoplodon bahamondi*) (p. 116)
34. Unidentified beaked whale (*Mesoplodon* sp. 'A') (p. 117)
36. Shepherd's beaked whale (*Tasmacetus shepherdi*) (p. 118)
Other names: Tasman beaked whale, Tasman whale
37. Cuvier's beaked whale (*Ziphius cavirostris*) (p. 118)
Other names: Goose-beaked whale, goosebeak whale, Cuvier's whale

FAMILY: DELPHINIDAE
38. Pygmy killer whale (*Feresa attenuata*) (p. 119)
Other names: slender blackfish, slender pilot whale
39. Melon-headed whale (*Peponocephala electra*) (p. 120)
Other names: little killer whale, electra dolphin, melonhead whale, many-toothed blackfish